A Window (

Eight Walks in
by
Kirsten Elliott

Illustrations by Jim Alcock
Maps by Kirsten Elliott

Guinea Lane, with (from left to right) houses prior to the landslip, Walcot Church, and The Star. From an early 19th-century print

Thanks are due to the many people who have helped with this book: first of all, my family and friends, particularly my long-suffering husband Steve, for having had to live with the whole project for over six months, and being dragooned into checking the routes for 'walkability' (which includes checking that my lefts and rights were sorted out); my mother also allowed me to plunder her extensive collection of books on Bath.

In addition, I would like to thank all those who so generously helped me with information, sharing research and documents with me. These include: Jim Cantello, Peter Davenport of Bath Archaeological Trust, Mike Davis at Independent Motors, John Ede, Trevor Fawcett, Marta Inskip, Colin Maggs, Jean Manco, George Moger, staff at The Paragon School (including Bill the groundsman), members of the U3A Local History Group in Lansdown, Christopher Woodward at the Building of Bath Museum, and all the other people who gave me snippets that have found their way into this book. Bath Reference Library and the Mayor's Honorary Guides' own library were valuable sources of research. Above all, however, this book is dedicated to

Colin Johnston and Mary Blagden at Bath City Archives Office

without whose patient help and advice this book would not have been possible.

First published in 1994 by
Millstream Books, 7 Orange Grove, Bath BA1 1LP

© Text and maps, Kirsten Elliot 1994
© Illustrations, Jim Alcock 1994

Set in Janson Text by Ryburn Publishing Services,
Keele University Press, Staffordshire

Printed by The Matthews Wright Press, Chard

ISBN 0 948975 38 5

Introduction

Using this book: It should be possible to follow the route of each walk by following the text, but in case you get lost, there is a map with each one. The exception is No.7, where you have to rely on the old maps provided instead. 18th-century spellings of street names were not consistent, and there is still some confusion, such as at Russel Street, which the Council likes spelt with two L's. I opt for the version carved into the stonework, with the exception of Rivers Street, which had a spurious apostrophe added before the S. I have tried not to use technical terms without explaining them, but I hope I have avoided being patronising. Your constant companion will be John Wood, whose description of Bath is an invaluable source of information. Wood was locally born, became a joiner and went off to London to serve his apprenticeship. He gradually turned builder and finally architect, before returning to Bath with his head full of great plans to build a new Rome. Like The Eternal City, Bath was in a valley ringed by seven hills. It was not to be. As his book makes obvious, Wood did not have the diplomatic skills necessary to ingratiate himself with the right people. In fact, he was irascible, opinionated, and full of himself. Yet his book, whose principal object seems to have been to denigrate all those who failed to recognise his talents, is, in an odd way, rather charming.

I also refer to Savile's, Speed's, and Gilmore's maps. Until 1992, Speed's map of 1612 was considered to be the oldest map of the city, with the exception of Smith's, which is more of a sketch. Then Savile's map was discovered, dated at about 1600. Although still rather controversial, most map experts now consider it to be genuine, and the one which Speed copied. The detail is magnificent, and though still not to scale, it is considerably more accurate than Speed's. For that reason, this is the one to which I refer. Gilmore's map of 1694, which, like the other two, tries to be three-dimensional, shows a city ripe for expansion, with houses crammed within the walls. It is surrounded by illustrations of buildings of interest to tourists, such as the Abbey and the Baths, together with various lodging houses.

Contents

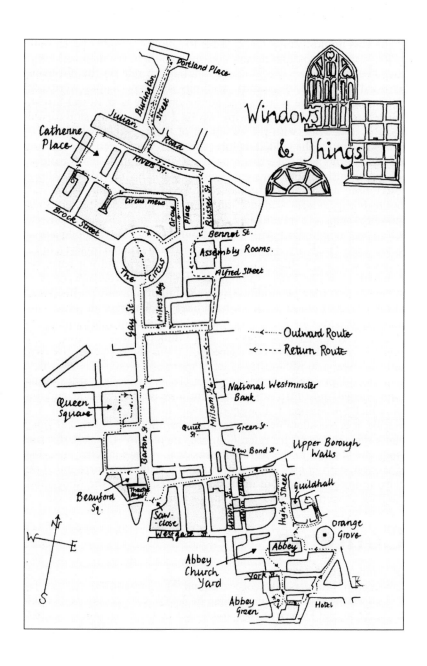

Windows & Things

Portland Place
Burlington Street
Julian Road
Catherine Place
Rivers St.
Circus mews
Brock Street
Gray Place
Russel St.
Bennet St.
Assembly Rooms.
Alfred Street
The Circus
Gay St.
Miles's Bdgs
········<···· Outward Route
·····<····· Return Route
Queen Square
Barton St.
National Westminster Bank
Milsom St.
Quiet St.
Green St.
New Bond St.
Upper Borough Walls
Guildhall
Beauford Sq.
Theatre Royal
Union St.
High Street
Orange Grove
Saw close
Westgate St.
Abbey
Abbey Church Yard
York St.
Hotel
Abbey Green

N
W E
S

Windows and Things

Why are we so interested in windows? To many of us they are the most important part of a building, and we will modernise our windows in line with the latest fashions. This has been going on through the centuries, as the walk will show. One of the most influential changes was the introduction of the sash window in the late 17th century. This came from Holland and although some sources attribute its name to the French word 'chassis', referring to its mechanics contained in a box in the window frame, Dutch architects say it came from their word for a sluice gate, which it certainly resembles. It was so fashionable that even cottage dwellers wanted them, while for the great architects, its tidy appearance was ideal for the classically-inspired designs they were producing. Casement windows, on the other hand, cluttered the lines of the building on being opened.

Even today there are fashions in windows. The seventies were the heyday of the aluminium-framed window, whereas the eighties have seen a return to wooden frames, usually in a heavy brown. As this walk unfolds, you will be introduced to the fashions in windows mainly of the 18th and 19th centuries, though we shall begin with a medieval fashion. This does not, however, answer the question why windows are important to us. Perhaps it is because they are the eyes of a building. As with people, so a long slit-like window can make a house look unfriendly; well-proportioned windows can make us pleased with a building. We shall see this as we go around the city.

However, just in case windows become all too much of a good thing, en route this walk takes in other interesting but disregarded items such as roof tiles, drainpipes, bell pulls and coal-holes.

Start: With your back to the West Door of *Bath Abbey*, look around you at the variety of windows you can see just by standing in this one spot. *Marshal Wade's House*, which contains the National Trust shop, has sash windows, but with a mass of tiny panes, whereas other 18th-century buildings have larger panes. One, at the corner of the alleyway which leads northwards out of the Church Yard, even has false windows painted on it. (These will be explained later in the walk.) On your left, at the far end, the *Pump Room* has oval windows and great semicircular fanlights, while the Victorian extension has some curved windows. There are several shop fronts, all different, and if you now turn and look up, you will see the West Window of the *Abbey* looming above you, with its pointed Gothic arch. This is the earliest window in Abbey Church Yard, and to look at Gothic windows in more detail, we will move on. Go through the gap between the *Abbey* and the *Roman Baths*, and look up at the south side of the church.

Bath Abbey is sometimes called the Lantern of the West, or even the Lantern of England, because of the size of its windows. Four-sevenths of its surface is said to be glass. Today that does not strike us as

Section showing mechanism of sash windows: lead weights are to the right of the frame. From an exhibit in the Building of Bath Museum

particularly remarkable, because we are used to entire buildings made of glass; we forget what a problem windows were to early builders. Little is known of the Saxon church that stood roughly on this site, but judging by other buildings of that date, what windows it had were probably small and round-headed. To avoid the complication of a keystone in an arch, the entire semi-circular head was sometimes cut out of one piece of stone. By the time the Normans arrived, some Saxon work was quite sophisticated, but much must have been swept away when the Normans rebuilt in the style that we name after them but should properly be called Romanesque. It was frequently highly decorated, but still rather massive, and still using round-headed arches. We know that the Norman cathedral at Bath was in this style, for one piece of arcade survives internally above a Gothic window, in the chapel in the south-east corner. It was not until the 12th century that the pointed arch appeared. Originally these were single narrow 'lancets', but as time went on, builders grouped them in threes and fives to make a bigger window. The mullions between them were slimmed down and decorative tracery was introduced, which had the added advantage of holding stained glass firmly. Gradually cathedral stonemasons experimented with ways of making huge structures appear to soar effortlessly. (They were not always successful. Some churches show signs of later propping up, and modern congregations sometimes find themselves paying the price for an over-ambitious medieval design.) One result was that the window area expanded, and *Bath Abbey*, built right at the end of the Gothic period, is the culmination of this trend. This, combined with the fact that there are 52 windows, ensures that on a fine day the *Abbey* is filled with sunlight.

Let us leave the *Abbey*, but stay within the monastery precincts by walking south across York Street, and continuing down Church Street to Abbey Green. There is a lot to see here, especially how fashions in windows change. Look first at No.3, an old gabled house with rubble-stone walls. Like several of its neighbours it dates from the 17th century, is partly timber-framed, and would have had the sort of windows that are associated with the Cotswold area: casement windows with dripstone mouldings above them. When sash windows became fashionable, they were altered, and you may see the marks of that on the front, the work not having been carried out in the most sophisticated manner! The shops and houses to its right also have this countrified appearance, and on one next to the modern arch the stone frames project considerably from the wall. Look at the little house to its left and you will see why. Here the rubble-stone has been plastered over as it was originally, and now the framing decoration takes on its intended appearance.

In 1695 the Government introduced Window Tax, which was really a wealth tax. It was the number of windows that was important, not the size, and immediately people found ways of avoiding it. Later, in the 1740s, an amendment was introduced such that if a window was less than 12 inches from its neighbour the two counted as one. As a result, people moved their windows closer together. The detached house to the left of No.3 was refronted in the 18th century, with windows grouped to avoid tax. They really are under 12 inches apart – just!

While thinking about Window Tax, this is a good time to consider glass-making. (Glass, incidentally, was also taxed, along with bricks and many other building materials.) It was difficult for 18th-century glass-makers to make cheap plate glass suitable for windows. There was a way which involved blowing a bubble, cutting it open and flattening the sheet, but it picked up impurities. Here and there you can find old houses with this type of glass. The preferred method was to gather up a blob of hot glass and spin it, resulting in a disc of glass, with a lumpy bit in the middle where the pontil, or iron rod used for blowing, joined the glass. Panes from this crown glass, as it was called, were cut from the flat part of the disc, leaving the boss or 'bull's eye' in the middle, which, in order to save waste, would be sold off cheaply to poorer people for their cottage windows. Now these bull's eyes are sought after to give an

Spinning the 'table' in the manufacture of Crown Glass. From an illustration in L'Encyclopédie Diderot

air of antiquity, and you can buy modern ones specially made. You can spot crown glass in windows by its greenish colour, and by looking for the curved grain running across the pane. By the 1820s, however, technological improvements had been made in the 'cylinder' form of glass-making, and in 1838 Patent Cheap Plate Glass came on the market.

This leads us on to the Crystal Palace of 1851, and on the west side of the square there is a pub named after it (though unfortunately the sign portrays the later Palace, built at Sydenham). Glass Tax had been lifted six years previously and Window Tax was removed that very year. All this led to a desire for more light, now cheaply available. People began to lengthen their windows. Some put in the new plate glass, but those who could not afford this did it as cheaply as possible by simply tagging an extra bit on the bottom. You can see this on the windows in the block adjoining *Abbey House*. It is possible that this lengthening began even before the advent of cheap plate glass, for the fashion from about 1790 onwards was for bigger windows. To detect if windows have been lengthened, see if the real windows are longer than false windows such as those you notice on the west side of *Abbey House*. These are generally to disguise staircases, chimney stacks, etc., and keep the balanced appearance required in Palladian architecture. Usually they had windows painted on them, as you saw in Abbey Church Yard. They were never altered because that was needless expense.

Let us now look at an old shop front. To the north of the pub is a double bow window, with curved railings in front of the right-hand bow. The bow allowed more goods to go in the window and more people to look in at one time. To stop people falling into the 'area' in front of the basement, there had to be railings, and some call these curved ones crinoline railings. The idea was that the ladies would not crush their full skirts against them, causing the dresses to stick out at the back! Unfortunately, at the time these were installed, crinolines were not being worn. Security was as much a problem in the past as it is now, and most shops had shutters. Look around the top of the bow and you will see the groove where they were slotted in at night before being bolted together.

Just before you leave Abbey Green, take a quick look at two more recent fashions. Next to the pub door which faces up towards York Street there is an Art Nouveau window, dating, one assumes, from the turn of this century, and to bring us right up to the present time, you can see some aluminium-framed windows in the modern building above the arch. Now leave the Green by the passageway next to No.3. On the left-hand building are some of those Cotswold-style windows complete with dripstones. Shortly on your left you will see a courtyard which is roughly at the original ground level, which over the years has risen. Looking across the courtyard and up, you will observe sash windows with little square panes and thick glazing bars as you saw at *Marshal Wade's House*. This means they are early. As time went on, panes became larger and glazing bars thinner. Continue along this passage, noticing on the building to your left some windows disappearing into the pavement, a relic of the earlier level. You then meet another passage.

You have now come into Gallaway's Buildings, or North Parade Buildings, as it has been rather prosaically renamed. Gallaway was an apothecary who developed this area about 1750 as possibly one of the earliest pedestrian precincts, wheeled vehicles being specifically excluded. There is a general set pattern to the houses, but the windows are rather uneven. Possibly this is due to the fact that Georgian developments were always carried out by numbers of builders who erected whatever they liked at the back, merely working to a set design for the façade. At the north-west end there are even round-headed windows. Looking at the front of the buildings on each side, you will see that there has been lengthening here, because the windows over some doorways cut down into the triangular pediments over the door. You will also notice a rich assortment of drain-pipes. Some come ruthlessly down the face of the house and are usually made of cast iron. These are additions in the 19th and early 20th centuries. One, however, still has the original lead pipe, held on to the wall with large flanges. You will see that it comes down between two houses rather than across the face of them, which would not have been acceptable. Ideally, no pipes came down the front of the building at all, and later we shall see how this was achieved.

Turning northwards you can see *Sally Lunn's House*. Despite the date on the plaque, this is actually no earlier than 1622, the frontage now being thought to be very early 18th-century. Here too, as you saw in Abbey Green, the windows have been arranged in pairs, to give six windows which only counted as three for Window Tax purposes. An easier way to dodge the tax can be seen by looking up at the building just to the right of *Sally Lunn's*: the owner simply blocked up a window. Looking further to your right you will notice the next building has a series of blank windows at the end. Like the ones in Abbey Green, but more importantly here, they were to preserve the architectural balance, despite a fireplace being behind them. However, in some parts of Bath there are false windows which are still Window Tax windows. Just as today you can either buy a basic car or pay more for optional extras, so in the Georgian period you could buy a house which had an adequate number of windows, but which had easily removable false ones. If you were prepared to pay for the luxury of more light, you could have it.

Assuming you want to leave *Sally Lunn's* interesting little museum for another time, turn right in front of the shop into what was once Lilliput Alley. Like Gallaway's Buildings it has suffered from unimaginative renaming and is now North Parade Passage. This will bring you out to North Parade. Look up at the *Compass Abbey Hotel* and you will see the drastic effect of cheap patent plate glass. Here every window of John Wood's development has been stripped of its glazing bars, ruthlessly lengthened and 'reveals' cut into the framing decoration, or architrave. Turn from this sorry sight towards *The Huntsman*, and you will see another Georgian shop front, here richly decorated. This was originally the Parade Coffee House. Looking up at a house in York Street, you can see some painted windows, now rather faded. In a house out along the London Road the false window has a false blind complete with pull-string, to add verisimilitude! Cross York Street and walk past the shops. Some have modern windows occasionally with overbearing fascia boards bearing the shop name: others have pretty Edwardian windows with graceful glazing bars decorated with flowers in the spandrels of the arches at the top. Turn the corner into Orange Grove and walk towards the east end of the *Abbey*, stopping where you can conveniently look up at the great East Window.

After what has already been said about the Gothic arch, you would expect this window to be the same, but surprisingly it is square-headed. Many reasons have been put forward for this, philosophical and practical, but whatever the reason, the 19th-century restorers were distinctly unhappy with it, and plastered over the spandrels (the roughly triangular shapes in the corners) in order to give back the Gothic shape. Fortunately, when the present window was installed in 1873, the spandrels were restored, but the sun and moon, the original decorations, were replaced with the more worthy coats of arms of Bath and the diocese. Stained-glass windows should really be seen from inside, and this one is well worth it, being 56 episodes from the life of Christ, designed by Clayton and Bell. Many Victorian church designs are over-sentimental, but these have an attractive story-book quality. Look out for the red and green devil. Some of the other windows are also by Clayton and Bell. Incidentally, the chancel is aligned so that on St. Peter's Day, the rays of the rising sun shine directly through the East Window.

Now walk along the north side of the *Abbey* and use the pedestrian crossing to cross the road. Once over, turn immediately right and walk along until you can look over to the shops on the other side of Orange Grove. These buildings are very early 18th-century – except for the façade! Originally they were similar in appearance to *Sally Lunn's*, but in the late 1890s they were refronted. The windows on the upper floors have a most curious arrangement of glazing bars. Is it Chinoiserie? If so, it sits rather oddly with the pseudo-Queen Anne shell canopies, not that a mixture of styles worried Victorian architects. Is it meant to look antique? Perhaps it was simply meant to be a pretty pattern – which it is. Now take the second passageway on your left, by the telephone box. It brings you out at the back of the *Guildhall*.

Face the *Guildhall* and look at the row of windows on the first floor (second floor if you are a transatlantic visitor!). These give light to the very beautiful Banqueting Room in the 18th-century part of the *Guildhall*, the architect being Thomas Baldwin. However, the central one, under the triangular pediment, has a rather blank appearance. It is another false window. Behind it is a fireplace. Although it is central, and hence a gap would not destroy the balance, the blank might draw the eye to the centre, and the viewer of Palladian buildings was meant to take in the design as a unified whole. So in went a false window. If there is a fireplace, there must be a chimney, and by looking at the roof-line you will see it, disguised by Baldwin as a sacrificial altar draped with garlands. In winter, the altar would have been smoking nicely.

We now have a slightly longer walk to look at our next windows and to take us clear of the busy shopping area. Retrace your steps, turning right to go round to the front of the *Guildhall*. (If you have time, you could see if the Banqueting Room is open to the public; it is well worth the detour.) Cross to the other side of High Street, turn right, and then left down Upper Borough Walls. Notice the shop-front on the right-hand side of the road, on the corner of New Bond Street Place. This has an interesting angular design dating from the 1920s. En route to the far end of Upper Borough Walls, see if you can spot the octagonal window with a little central octagon which opens independently of the rest of the window. To give you a clue, it is up quite high on your right, as you pass the *Mineral Water Hospital*.

Arriving in the Sawclose car park, we shall begin by looking at a modern building, although you may not recognise it as such. It is over to your left: the row of colonnaded shops known as *Seven Dials*. This appears to be based on the works of a local architect of the early 19th century called Pinch: the way in which the cornice sweeps upwards to hide the stepping effect on a hill is very characteristic. It is one of the finest modern buildings in Bath, but rather severe. Pinch's buildings often have some added decoration such as a Vitruvian scroll above or below the first floor windows, or architectural detail around the windows. Today, of course, that would have been extra expense because, while materials are comparatively cheap, labour is expensive. In the Georgian period it was the other way around.

Turn now to the pub *The Garrick's Head*, which was the home of Richard 'Beau' Nash, the most famous of Bath's Masters of Ceremonies. This house is dated at 1720, and is an attempt by a local builder called Greenway to emulate the Palladian style. You can tell it is early by the little square panes of glass in the sashes, in an arrangement called 'nine over nine'. It has the thick glazing bars you would expect to find for a house of this date. Now walk past the theatre entrance and *Popjoy's Restaurant*, and turn left into Beauford Square. Looking at the houses on the northern side, and bearing in mind what you now know, you can have a good guess at the history of this row. See if you can work it out before reading the next paragraph.

Some of the houses have nine over nine windows, therefore they are of early date (1730s). Originally they all had architraves but when the 12-inch rule came in for Window Tax, most were moved. Some owners did it cheaply and kept the old frames, but some took the opportunity to switch to the more fashionable six over six arrangement, with rectangular panes and thinner glazing bars. This is the classic 18th-century window, its panes in proportion to the window, and the window in proportion to the building. Did you get it right? What makes these frames particularly interesting is that they retain the wedges which could be pegged to prevent the window slipping. Ideally this should not occur; the lead weights in the mechanism should match the weight of the window precisely so that they are always balanced. If, however, for some reason the weights went missing, the sash window could be a dangerous and painful object, as readers of *Tristram Shandy* will know. Now continue westwards, turn sharp right at the corner into Princes Street and go to the end.

You are now in Queen Square, named after Queen Caroline, wife of George II. Cross the road carefully (this has become a roundabout, albeit an elegant one) and go into the gardens in the centre. Walk up to the northern side and look at John Wood's palace front. Alas, here too the windows have been lengthened. The original design had balustraded pedestals below the first-floor windows but these have, unfortunately, disappeared. Does lengthening matter? Queen Square is the best place to prove that it does. Walk round to the eastern side. Here are two houses which have had the windows restored, and between them, one which has not. You can tell the windows were lengthened because the window goes through the sill band, a narrow course of blocks which allowed the sills to stand out. (If you are not sure if lengthening has occurred, look for this giveaway sign.) The windows are the same width as those on each side, but look much narrower. Worse than that, the whole house looks narrower, simply because the proportions, which were so important to Palladian architects, have been destroyed. Not all windows had an equal number of panes in the upper and lower frames. In order to make the windows on the second floor less important, John Wood sometimes designed them shorter, but kept the width of three panes. Some upper frames, therefore, have three panes and not six.

Moving into the south-east corner, look to the left across the road at Northumberland Buildings. These are later, by Thomas Baldwin, and are in the Neo-classical rather than the Palladian style. See how much lighter the decoration is than on the north side of the square. Excavations at places such as Pompeii had revealed that the Romans sometimes used this style, particularly for domestic buildings. This change in fashion did not stop the Victorians from altering the windows just as ruthlessly. A quick look at the false side windows will reveal the truth, although some have, happily, been restored. This terrace is sometimes criticised for its rather heavy attic storey, but window-lengthening has accentuated it. The original windows were tiny oblongs, as the blind ones show, but increasing their size has made the whole attic floor more dominant. However, one has to agree that the servants who slept in the garrets must have welcomed the extra light. A bit of comfort would not have come amiss; the attics were hot in summer and cold in winter. Now leave Queen Square, making your way over to the pavement on the eastern side and then up to Gay Street. As you reach the top corner of the square, look at No.41, the one with a curved window. The window has a curved frame to go with it, a most unusual feature for such an early date (1735). Generally this is an indication of a house of the 1800s. Windows are normally for looking out, but you may look into the next window of No.41, on the south side of the door, to see the powder room. This was not for ladies, but for gentlemen to go and powder their wigs. Continue up Gay Street and turn right into George Street. At No.11 George Street, a chemist's, there is a magnificent Art Nouveau shop window, dating from 1907. The decorative lights are bevelled plate glass. Apparently, it is now almost impossible to replace them if they are damaged.

You now need to cross the road, the best way being to take the extra time to go past Milsom Street and up to the pedestrian-controlled lights. Turn left and walk along the raised pavement until you come to the passageway called Miles's Buildings, where we are going to have a short break from windows. If you walk up until you are opposite No. 8, you will notice some square stones with small central holes let into the paving. These are coal-holes. Beneath your feet are cellars, as indeed there are nearly everywhere you walk in Georgian Bath. They were used for storing many things, including wine and items to be kept cool such as game. Principally they were for coal, and since house-owners did not want the coalman walking in through the front door or even through the garden and kitchens, the simple method was to insert a coal-hole in the pavement. The coalman had a gadget he would put through the hole in the centre, remove the stone and shoot the coal straight down. The parlour maid would then come through a door below the front door into the cellars, where she could collect the coal to light your fire. Today these covers are usually replaced with metal plates, but Bath is fortunate to have some of these original stone covers still remaining.

Returning to windows, you should begin to retrace your steps, but as you get to the lamp-post near the end of Miles's Buildings look up to your left. Here the triple grouping with the arched central light is called a Venetian window. The added attraction of these to Georgian tax-payers was that the slim mullions gave three windows for the price of one. In one the glazing bars are arranged in the 'Gothick' style, a charming if incorrect use of the medieval idiom, popularized by Horace Walpole at Strawberry Hill. Turn right along the high pavement and right again up Gay Street. Notice the 'Carved House' (No.8) on the left side of the street. The first lease-holder was Prince Hoare, a sculptor, and he seems to have demanded something a bit more fancy than the rest of the street. Now keep climbing until you reach The Circus, where you should begin by standing in the centre.

This, surely, is a truly Georgian building, with the elaborate carving and pretty balconies. Or is it? Again the false windows at the side give the game away. Every single one of the first floor windows has been lengthened, and the pretty balconies are in fact window guards, added to stop people, their children and their pets from falling out. Now cross to No.14 in the northern segment. This has an ironwork archway with a basket and is called an overthrow. This was 18th-century street lighting. Between 14th September and 25th March each year, every household had to "hang out Candles or Lights, in Lanthorns, on the

Outside of their respective Houses ... for the Conveniency of Passengers ... until Twelve at Night". The overthrow would contain a lamp, put there at night by a servant. To do so, he had to climb a ladder, and this overthrow still retains the bracket where the ladder could rest without slipping. Move in a clockwise direction until you come to No.17, the home of Thomas Gainsborough. At the back of the house, out of sight of the public, there has been some more window-lengthening, but this happened in the 1760s, when Gainsborough had it done to let more light into his painting room. There is an object of interest at the front, however. Look at the little gateway which leads down into the area. Just beside it you can see a gadget with a knob, now no longer connected to anything. (A chain has recently been installed but not joined up. This is probably how it worked.) It is a bell pull for tradesmen. As you can see, the tradesman's entrance was down a flight of steps to the door beneath the front door, thus to save his legs, the door bell was put at street level. The cook or housekeeper could come out to see what he wanted, and only if it was absolutely necessary would he have to plod down all the steps.

Leave The Circus by the eastern exit and turn immediately left into Circus Place. Go up and around the corner, and about 50 yards along stand where you can easily look back at the old cottages past which you have come as well as at the modern buildings on each side. The old buildings have clearly undergone modernisation, but it has been done sensitively. There is nothing pretentious about them. They are good, honest buildings, but that in itself is attractive. Now look ahead at the modern houses. There are two approaches here. On one side, Circus Mews copies the solid appearance of the old houses; if anything the arrangement of the windows is rather too solid, but to be fair, these houses really face on to the inner courtyard. On the other side, at Nash Gardens, there is a perfect extravaganza of windows: long, short, at different levels, dormer windows, and some with curved tops which sit rather uneasily with the straight eaves. To cap it all off there is a little belfry – with no bell! This building awakens strong emotions in people: they either love it or loathe it. It must be the windows; in all other respects it is a perfectly normal structure.

Continue along the street until on your left you see an insignificant street (also called Circus Place) which takes you to the back of Brock Street and The Circus. Here you can see why it is said that Bath's buildings are Queen Anne in front and Mary Ann behind! But amongst this muddle you can spot some more Georgian Gothick windows. However, the purpose of being here is to find out how Georgian builders avoided down-pipes at the front. The rainwater would gather in drains at the front of the house, and if it was a double mansard roof, it would gather in the middle as well. From there it was channelled into a wooden gutter, lined with lead but open at the top, which ran (or rather runs, because these houses still have them) right through the roof space before coming out of a spout at the back. Sometimes there is a pipe, sometimes a lead-lined 'mouth', and sometimes a tile simply appears to be missing. Look up at the steep part of the roofs and you may be able to spot them. Owners of period houses will tell you that while this sounds like a good idea, in practice it is a bit like having a rather unpredictable stream running through the attic.

Go back to Circus Mews and turn left. As you enter Catharine Place, look to your left down the wide passageway known as Margaret's Buildings. The first two shop-fronts on the left show how well some modern architects deal with designing in a conservation area. Continue along the south side of Catharine Place to a small alleyway on the left which takes you down to some lock-up garages. If you look up at the roofs of the houses in Brock Street you will notice that one still has its Cotswold stone tiles at the top, and clay pantiles on the lower part. In the 17th century nearly all houses would have been tiled like this, and at first this continued into the Georgian period. Slate, with its smooth appearance, became more fashionable, but was expensive. So even quite late in the 18th century some builders economised by putting slate at the front and stone tiles at the back.

Return to Catharine Place and make your way up the western side, watching out for examples of lengthening, including some done on the cheap. Here and there you may notice where the internal shutters had to have an extra piece added at the same time. These internal shutters were as much for security as for keeping the night air out. Smashing windows seems to have been the favoured form of vandalism throughout the Georgian period, as the newspapers confirm. Even Richard Nash, when he had lost badly at the gaming tables is said by Lady Bristol to have "broke all the windows according to custom". Turn right along the top of Catharine Place, which is Rivers Street, and then first left. At the top, directly opposite on the other side of Julian Road, you will see a strange modern block that obviously set out to look Palladian but fails. No Palladian building ever had an arrangement of windows like that. The heavy wooden frames tell you it was built in the 1980s.

The furthest point of the walk is now in sight. Walk up Burlington Street until you reach Portland Place. Climb up to the raised pavement, the slopes being chair ramps for sedan chairs as well as wheeled ones. Windows were getting bigger by the 1780s, so are the ones in the central house original or have they been lengthened? Look for the sill band. At some time verandas have been added to the terrace, though one has since disappeared again. The two overthrows are original, and when new must have been very fine, with their beautiful scrolled ironwork. Another feature to look at are fanlights over the doors, in the Adam style. The nearer they get to the central door, the more decorative they become. Looking down Burlington Street, you will see that some houses have had wooden sunshades added above the windows some time in the 19th century. To your left, one of the houses in the block at an angle has arched windows. These may be an alteration, except that another house on the right-hand block has similar windows hidden away at the back. Perhaps this was an experiment by the builders. Also on the right-hand block you can see a Window Tax 'pair' at a corner, and to the right of that there are some very strange window alterations. Some of the front doors still have the little window beside them through which the footman could take a peep at callers. Now compare the old buildings with the blocks built in the 1960s, of which there are examples to right and far left. This kind of architecture is now regarded with disfavour; the fenestration, or arrangement of windows, does nothing to enhance it. The block to the right sits most uncomfortably with its older neighbour, unlike the Victorian house to the west of Portland Place. Although in a very different style, it is still a well-mannered building in its setting.

Return: Go back down Burlington Street, noticing the rather peculiar triple windows (one can hardly call them Venetian) on the left-hand side. The church on the right, by the way, was designed by the firm of Dunn and Hansom, of whom it was said that Dunn saw that it was handsome, and Hansom saw that it was done. Go back the way you came, but turn left when you get to Rivers Street. This was too expensive for Fanny Burney and her emigré husband Count d'Arblay, but when the window was lengthened on the octagonal bow that looks down Russel Street, it was still done by the cheap method. Go down Russel Street, turn right and then left in front of the Assembly Rooms into Alfred Street. Alfred House has an overthrow complete with link-snuffers, where the link-boys who ran in front of the sedan chairs at night put out their flaming torches (or 'links'). Next to the overthrow there is a hoist for lowering goods into the kitchens and cellars, while at No.13 there is a boot-scraper near the door (18th-century streets were very mucky). Turn left, and then right down the passage between the antique markets. Notice the florid 19th-century shop-fronts in red marble to your right. When you reach George Street, look diagonally to your left across to Bladud Buildings. They date from 1755, but the curved frame to the windows in the bow round the corner tells you that it is a later addition. Cross and make your way down Milsom Street. Here you are surrounded by shop windows in which you may be tempted to gaze, but instead, look in the window of the National Westminster Bank, and admire the ceiling of the banking hall. The bank authorities will have no objection if you want to take a closer look by going inside. And so this walk ends, leaving you looking through a window.

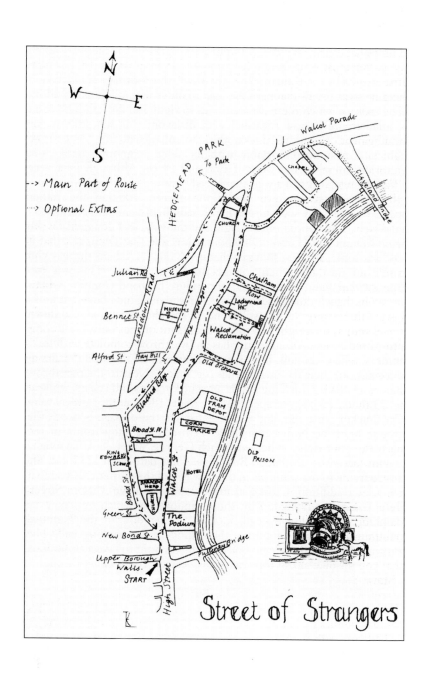

Street of Strangers

Street of Strangers

This walk takes in an old part of the city which existed outside the City Wall. For most of its history, Bath was contained within the defences first erected by the Romans. If not true walls at that time, they certainly became so as the Romans left and war made strong defences necessary. The entire city lay in the bottom of the valley, the wall being less than a mile around, with just three streets outside. To the south was Southgate or Horse Street, and to the north were Walcot and Broad Streets. It is these two streets and the area near them through which this walk will take us.

Various explanations are given for the name Walcot, but one is that when the Saxons arrived sometime in the 6th century they noticed that it had been heavily settled by the Romano-British. The Anglo-Saxons rather cheekily called the Celts foreigners or strangers, for which their word was *welisc* or *wealh*. From this we get *Wal*es, Corn*wall*, and *Wal*cot. We are fortunate that the street is still there to be explored, which would not be the case had the Abercrombie or Buchanan plans ever been carried out. The former was a postwar idea for modernising Bath. It involved such radical ideas as taking over the Royal Crescent as the Civic Offices and Norfolk Crescent for the Technical College. In the event, only the bus station and the abattoir were ever built, which was just as well, because one part of the plan was to sweep away Walcot Street entirely and put in a Neo-georgian block, with a road running alongside the river. In 1964, Colin Buchanan and Partners produced a report on traffic which suggested carrying cross-city traffic under Bath in a tunnel, access being in Royal Victoria Park and Walcot Street. Once again parts of the area hung under the threat of demolition, though to be fair to Buchanan, it was the Council's amendments to his plan which were potentially so destructive.

While the Council debated, the conservation lobby, aghast at the destruction of many old parts of Bath, was beginning to be heard. In 1973, Adam Fergusson published *The Sack of Bath* and the year before Peter Coard had published the less sensational, but in many ways more damning, *Vanishing Bath*. The effects could be seen in the report published by the Council in 1978. It was called *Saving Bath – A Programme for Conservation*. It is as a result of that change in thinking that you are able to carry out this walk today.

Start: Begin on the corner of Upper Borough Walls and Northgate Street. For a moment try to blot out the traces of three centuries. There is certainly no modern traffic, but gone too are all the 18th-century buildings. You are standing in the north-east corner of the old walled city, with the wall in front of you. Immediately to your right is the North Gate, and beside it an old church being used both as a prison and a school. Beyond the walls are fields and orchards with, to east and south, the river. Through the North Gate is the way out of the city towards London, along Walcot Street. This route has been used since Roman times; it is possible that it is the Fosse Way, though its course through Bath is not certain. Bring yourself back to the present and make your way across to the *Podium*. In doing so, you can see a very old, narrow route to the river, now blocked at the far end. It runs between two shops on the east side of Northgate Street. Stand in the wide space outside the *Podium*. You have now stepped outside the old city and into a district that was noted for trade, especially weaving.

From where you are standing, your view up Walcot Street is blocked by part of the *Podium* development. Unfortunately the 1978 plan came too late to save the first piece of Walcot Street, and the *Beaufort Hotel* went on the site. By the eighties this had become an officially ugly building, and one of the requirements for the developers of the *Podium* site was that they should hide the *Beaufort* as much as possible. The result is felt by some to be nearly as bad, though much of the problem is caused by the pillars outside the supermarket which appear to be of a new order: 'sewer-pipe-ian'. Inside, however, it is rather jolly. The main *Post Office*, on the other side of the street, was built in the 1930s, and is a thoughtful piece of Neo-georgian. Ugly buildings are not a prerogative of the 20th century, and the church which stands in the fork between Broad Street and Walcot Street replaces one that received tremendous criticism throughout the Georgian period and lasted less than a hundred years.

The church is dedicated to St. Michael, and is properly called *St. Michael's Without*, or St. Michael Extra Muros, because it was outside the walls. There has been a church here since at least the 13th century. In 1581, the Council needed lead to repair the pipes which brought water to the conduits. The lead was therefore removed from the church roof and it was tiled instead. With treatment like this, it is not too surprising that by 1730 it was almost ruinous, and John Wood offered to build a new one at his own expense, provided he could retain the old materials and have some pews set aside for residents of his newly-completed Queen Square. Reading between the lines one suspects that the Vestry committee thought this rather high-handed, and said if he felt like that he could go away and build his own church for Queen Square (which he duly did). Instead, in 1734, a new church was put up by the church warden, Harvey, "in a Taste so peculiar to himself," said John Wood, "that the very Journeymen Workmen to mortify him declared that a Horse, accustomed to the Sight of good Buildings, was so affrighted at the odd Appearance of the Church that he would not go by it till he was hoodwinked". By the early 1800s opinions had not changed. "Economy was preferred to taste and beauty of design," said Pierce Egan in 1819. "It was an annoyance to admirers of architecture in Bath." It was a relief, therefore, when in 1835 Manners built the present church in the Early English style, influenced by Salisbury Cathedral. It was a pity his work on the Abbey was not as graceful as this. The church is unusual in being orientated north/south, as was

Harvey's. The site *is* very cramped, but the old church managed to sit across it. Its churchyard has disappeared under the modern developments on your right, along with rows of little houses which had quaint names like Hen and Chicken Court.

Continue up Walcot Street. Just after passing the end of the *Podium* you will see on your right what seems to be a kind of garden folly, with plants growing over it. It is, in fact, the air vent for the car park beneath, and is an enormous improvement on its slab-like predecessor. Moving on a little further, you can see the *Beaufort*, or *Bath Hilton Hotel* as we must now call it. Among the collection of buildings and courts which stood here previously was a pub called *The Three Cups*, part of an earlier inn, *The Pelican*. It was a large hostelry with stabling for 40 horses, and was where Dr. Johnson stayed when he came to Bath. There was a plaque to commemorate this, but even this has vanished. There were so many pubs in Walcot Street it was sometimes said that there was one in every other house. This is something of an exaggeration, but it was not short of them, and nor was Broad Street. However, Pierce Egan describes it as entirely devoted to shops and trade. Despite a certain amount of tidying, it still has a pleasingly raffish air. Much of the trade was due to the presence of the market, and by walking on until nearly opposite the *YMCA*, you will bring yourself into the market area.

The charter for a market was granted by Edward III in 1317. By the early 19th century, if not earlier, the market had spilled out into the street itself. Photographs from the 1890s show the sheep pens and some of the pubs. Repeated efforts were made by the Council to

The market in Walcot Street, circa 1900

prevent this happening. The *Corn Market*, with its row of arches, was erected in the early 19th century, and is described as having "secure granaries for safely lodging such corn as may remain for disposal to an ensuing day; the vaults beneath communicate with the river, and are well calculated for wholesome slaughter-houses". More improvements took place in 1855, when the newspaper referred to untidy sheds on the site, with most transactions being conducted in pubs. A new market hall was built roughly where you are standing. In the process a wheelwright's shop and a tripe-boiler's shop had to be replaced, giving some idea of the nature of this area. All around were businesses associated with the market, such as slaughter-houses, malthouses, stables, etc. There was another pub about here, *The Newmarket Tavern*, and on the opposite side of the road, *The King's Head*.

Looking across the river, you will notice what appears to be an elegant Palladian house but was actually the prison. It was part of a deal struck between the Council and the Pulteney family, who wanted to develop their estates on the other side of the river. The Pulteneys wished to build a bridge and a street leading to it, but the church being used as a prison was in the way. (The school had moved by this time, and later we shall see where it went.) If, said the Council cunningly, the Pulteneys wanted to take over this site, they would have to construct a new prison, designed by the City's favourite architect, Thomas Atwood. By strange coincidence he was also a councillor. The agreement was made in 1765, but it was not until 1772 that the foundation stone was laid in what is now Grove Street. It was just 60 feet by 30, and even in the 18th century this was considered a touch small for a prison, especially since it was to include debtors. However, this seems to have resulted in it having such a fearful reputation that it kept the crime rate down. It was built in the same way that most houses in Bath were constructed. What were to become the basements were built at ground level, with the rest of the house correspondingly one floor up. The vaulted street was then constructed in front, so now all the floors were in the right place. As there were, at the time, no other buildings in the street, the approach was erected where it was estimated the rest of the roadway would be eventually. Unfortunately, when Grove Street was finally built, it was lower than first thought – one whole floor lower. The roadway in front of the prison was demolished, with the result that the 'basements' are now at ground level and the 'ground floor' sits one floor up. From where you are, you see it as it was intended to be seen, but the front door has had to be turned into a window.

Also from here you have a good view of *Sham Castle*, the little eye-catcher up on the skyline, among the trees. Built by Ralph Allen in 1762, it was to give unadulterated nature a more picturesque effect. It was possibly inspired by the fake castle at Stowe, but that at least has a cottage lurking behind it. This one has nothing at all; it is simply a wall, a complete fake or "sham", hence its popular name. Its correct name, however, is the *Castle on the Warren*.

Turning your attention back to Walcot Street, walk past the entrance to the *Corn Market* and look at the brick building set back just beyond it. This is the old depot and power station for the trams, and stands in Beehive Yard, partly on the site of a malthouse and partly on the site of Walcot Foundry. Horse trams were introduced into the city in 1879, but in 1901 the Bath and District Light Railway Company was formed to introduce electric trams. Work on the permanent way began in Walcot Street in 1902, the labour force being provided by unemployed men in the city. They were paid 4½d. a day, and worked for 12 hours. The company changed its name and management and became Bath Electric Tramways Limited, a name it retained long after it only ran buses and had been merged with other companies. It finally disappeared into the puzzlingly-named Badgerline Bus Company. The foundry continued in existence until the 1970s. There are items around the city, such as coal-hole covers, which still bear its name.

The Beehive Yard was the stable yard for another pub, not surprisingly called *The Beehive*. Its buildings are the next ones you come to after the entrance to the yard. On market days the sheep pens were right up against its walls, and it was popular with farmers. Almost next to it was *The Catherine Wheel* which at the turn of the century advertised "well-aired beds". Looking to your left you can see the backs of two sets of 18th-century terraces, Bladud Buildings and The Paragon. Both are unusual in having double elevations, that is to say, they are as smart at the back as they are at the front. This particularly applies to Bladud Buildings, the row nearest to you. They were built in 1755 on a site formerly known as either Cockey's Garden or the Town Garden. The Paragon is later, dating from 1769, and was designed by Thomas Atwood. Atwood usually (and deservedly) gets a bad press. He was devious and corrupt, nemesis finally catching up with him in 1775 when he died as the result of a fall through the floor of an old house in the market place. But his work on The Paragon is a clever use of a difficult site. He had to shore up the ground with extensive vaults and retaining walls. These were used as coach-houses and for storage, and you will see them on your left as you walk along. Although the entrances to the houses face on to the road above (you will see them later on), you are really looking at the front from this side. Internally, the normal arrangement of rooms and staircases has been turned around, so that the principal rooms can enjoy the view.

Walcot Street is very wide at this point, and by walking a little further you will find yourself opposite an elaborate horse trough, now used in the Floral City as a plant container. It was given by Miss Elizabeth Landon, designed by Major Davis, and was "composed of specimens from all the various building stones found in the immediate neighbourhood, with the addition of granite and white marble introduced with reference to colour. The design ... is a most harmonious composition." (From a guide to Bath, 1864.) The trough, with its wide curve where cattle could drink, also contained a fountain

23

for humans, but it seems the two-legged animals preferred a different tipple. The 1886 OS map gives it as the site of the old Carn Well. John Wood describes this as "issuing out of a Spout in the back Wall of an Alcove, formerly placed upon the West Side of Waldcot Street … and stood a small matter within the North End of St. Michael's Parish". He goes on to say that it disappeared due to road widening – even then Walcot's history fell victim to the demands of traffic. Although the parish boundary is some way up the street, the road is certainly wide here, so this may well be the right place. The spring was supposed to be especially good for curing eye disorders.

On the right-hand side of the street is *St. Michael's Church House*, one of Bath's very few pieces of Art Nouveau architecture. It was built in 1904, designed by Wallace Gill. A balletic St. Michael, straight from the pages of Aubrey Beardsley, can be seen over the door. Next to it is a little lane called Old Orchard. Turn down here, and as you walk down you will notice a door to a snooker club called the *Red House*. This is a relic from the days when this was all part of The Old Red House Bakery, founded in 1798 by Alfred Taylor. The shop, which was painted crimson, was in New Bond Street. Now continue to the bottom of the lane where you will find a most attractive row of cottages. These were recently restored, and rightly so. Though they were quite humble homes, they have great charm. Built in the late 18th century, they show windows grouped in pairs to avoid Window Tax (see 'Windows and Things') and a long timber beam called a 'bressumer' right across the front. It should properly be lime-washed to disguise its presence, and is there because the walls of these houses are a single block deep. This sort of construction was liable to move after completion, and the timber would absorb it. It had the added advantage that the front could be kept open allowing building materials to be brought in without difficulty. The front wall would be added at the end. At present the fashion is to reveal these bressumers, and even stain the timber brown – the Georgian builders would be horrified!

Return to Walcot Street and turn right, the building on the corner once being yet another pub, *The Bladud's Head*. It was here that the City Fathers came for a celebratory lunch, having opened the new market hall in 1855. Ironically, one of its purposes was to dissuade farmers from doing business in a pub! The next building was the bakery, opened in 1903. Continuing northwards along the street, we come to *Walcot Reclamation*. This was the yard of some local builders, Hayward and Wooster, but is now a fascinating collection of rescued artefacts all looking for a new home – at a price! Old roof tiles and floorboards are just as much antiques as anything you may see in Bath's many antique shops, and *Walcot Reclamation* has been in business now for over 15 years. If the yard is open, walk in and take a look. If you want anything from a lamp-post to a pair of Ionic columns, you will find it here.

You should also take the opportunity to walk right down through the yard to the river (Warning – the steps are *very* steep) and turn left.

Climb the steps now facing you and look up at the building whose gardens run down to the river. This is now called *Ladymead House*, although strictly speaking you have almost left the part of Walcot Street known as Lady Mead. One reason given for the name is that the land was owned by Edith, wife of Edward the Confessor. There was a house here from at least 1661, and a painting in the Victoria Art Gallery purports to show it and its gardens. Before the 18th century there were many gardens like this by the river, and some feel that they can still see the remnants of those painted gardens in what you see today. The building became known as Cornwell House, a corruption of the name Carn Well. In 1805 it was turned into a penitentiary where "46 females of fallen reputation should find shelter, advice, and encouragement to return to the paths of virtue". To it was added in 1816 that ominous-sounding institution, a Lock Hospital, where "the severe illness of several have been solaced by the kindest care and attention; and the dying hours of some victims of vice and folly soothed". The penitentiary had mixed success: some were taught housework and needlework and placed in gainful employment, but others escaped and some were expelled for disorderly conduct. It is now sheltered accommodation for elderly ladies, an institution of a very different kind. Return through the yard, and as you turn the corner into Walcot Street you will see the elegant offices of Hayward and Wooster, the firm founded in 1840. They are now all part of *Walcot Reclamation*.

You will then be about to pass the street elevation of *Ladymead House*, but as you do so, look down at the base of the wall where you will find the letters WP and St. MP. These are parish boundary marks. You are about to leave St. Michael's Parish and enter Walcot – as long as you stay on this side of the road. There was once a water-course here that divided the two parishes. The northern side of *Ladymead House* is by James Wilson, erected when improvements were made to the Penitentiary chapel. In 1825, the Lock Hospital was converted by Manners to a chapel, which could seat 300 in addition to the penitents. This was made possible by a Mr. Parish, a great benefactor to the charity. He was also involved with the Bath and Bathforum Free School, founded in 1810, which was the first school open to all poor children. It was non-denominational, and for a few years from 1823 it adjoined the penitentiary. Peter Coard, in *Vanishing Bath*, places it at the shop next door but it is more likely it was in the buildings at the back (some of which were leased by the penitentiary) which later became a pin manufactory, pin-making being a common local industry. The shop (Nos.114–116) was at one time another pub, *The Walcot Wine Vaults*. It has a most unusual concave façade which was necessary to allow coaches to turn into the stable yard on the other side of the road.

Take the next turning on your right, which is Chatham Row. This was called Pitt Street when it was first built in 1762, and was named after William Pitt, then MP for Bath. Four years later he was made Earl of Chatham, and Bath kept up with this by renaming the street. This small but delightful terrace was blighted for many years by the various schemes mentioned earlier. Indeed the house at the bottom with the Venetian window was used in 1967 by the Fire Brigade to test the fire resistant properties of 18th-century buildings. Readers will be glad to know that the results exceeded basic requirements. Fortunately they have been beautifully restored. In 1856, the bottom house was a soup kitchen, provided by the Society for Improving the Condition of the Working Classes in Bath. There were branches in poorer parts of the city, but this one also had a grocer's shop. Here too, the street is vaulted, with the cellars beneath. The coal-holes can be seen in the road, and the natural level of the ground can be seen by looking over the wall at the gardens. Just beyond the top couple of gardens, the wall has a bend in it, which dates back to when there was a filbert hedge there. Although the hedge had gone by 1779, the bend in the wall remains. Before you return to Walcot Street, look at the end house on the southern side. Houses in the various terraces in Bath were built by different builders, and you can see how one joined up to the next, because here the 'next' house never came into existence. Tooth stones were left jutting out of back and front walls, together with stones coming from the spine wall which ran across the middle of the house. They have been tidied up a bit, but the remains are still visible.

When you get to the top of Chatham Row you will see *The Bell*. This was a kind of coaching inn, where 'caravans', that is carts carrying goods and poorer passengers, arrived and departed. The stables which necessitated the curved shop-front belonged to this inn. It has been a pub since at least 1765, when the licensee was Peter Hooper, but he had leased the plot from the council before that. It is still very active! It is also the last house in St. Michael's Parish on the other side of the road: you can see the parish boundary mark St.MP at the far end. It is an odd fact that the bulk of Walcot Street is not in Walcot Parish at all. Once the second largest parish in England (a curious claim to fame) Walcot rose to prominence with the growth of Georgian Bath, the bulk of the New Town being within its bounds. 'Islands' of Walcot existed in neighbouring parishes. In 1863, when the parish held its 'Cuckoo Revels', a perambulation of the boundaries, it took two days. This was partly due to the fairly riotous nature of the exercise, with its frequent stops for food and drink. Walk on a little further until you have on your left a row of pretty 18th-century cottages, some of which still have the original glazing bars *and* the original glass. On your right is an auction house. This part of the parish was quite industrial by the 19th century, with the sort of housing to match. Two whole streets, now demolished, were squeezed into the space between Chatham Row and the auction house, built in 1904 as a new home for Walcot Schools. To do so, it was necessary to demolish the house which stood here, confusingly also known as Cornwell House. Frequently attributed to the Queen Anne period because of its shell doorway, it does not appear on maps until the 1790s. Notice, up to your right, the advertisements painted on the buildings (you may have seen some already). Modern advertising is quite restrained and tasteful compared with that of the 19th and early 20th centuries, when anything upright was seen as a potential billboard.

On the other side of the street you can now see the side of *Walcot Parish Church* (you will see the front later). The original foundation dates back over a thousand years, when Alphege established a church here, dedicated to St. Swithin. It was tiny, but so was the population until the 18th century. In 1777 the main part of the present church was built, with additions in 1788 and the spire in 1790. The architect, John Palmer, is buried there. Notice how the congregation was wealthy enough to afford ashlar blocks throughout the construction, and decoration along the sides. Burials took place in the crypt, the burial area beside the church, which included catacombs and then in the open space to your right. Walk a little way down the new road called Walcot Gate and stop outside the mortuary chapel, dated 1842, now trans-mogrified into *Walcot Village Hall*. Looking straight ahead you can see the side of *Walcot Chapel*, designed in 1815 for the Methodists by an itinerant preacher, the Reverend William Jenkins. Architects rather turn their noses up at it, but it is certainly more pleasing than some of the efforts from the 1960s. Here the congregation was not so wealthy, so there is rubble-stone construction at the sides, with no decoration. From here you can also see some remnants of the little houses that were crammed into this part of the city. Almost directly opposite is a house called *Terra Incognita*, which was probably part of George's Buildings, and now fortunately habitable, but further in the distance you can see two houses in a ruinous state. This is all that is left of St. Swithin's Place. These are actually listed buildings, but the *Saving Bath* plan described them as "of only secondary townscape interest" and recom-mended that they be cleared. Neglect seems to be achieving this end.

You can now make a choice. If you feel you have walked far enough from the city centre, go back up to Walcot Street and pick up the route again from the paragraph marked *, otherwise continue down the new road as it curves round to the right. In front of you is a new housing development. When this space was cleared, the archaeologists found a wealth of Roman relics. The cemetery also had to be cleared, which caused some controversy, for it was not done as carefully as it might have been, and some of the locals complained. There is no record of the dead having shown their displeasure, however. As you can see, some old names have been revived, as in Caern Well Place. Cross left through the car park in front of Nelson Buildings. Go up to the left just before the Methodist church car park, where you will find a path that takes you past the back of the chapel. Just before the path turns up to rejoin the road, look down towards the river, where you will see what looks like yet another chapel. It was an organ factory, and is now the Bath Canoe Centre. As you go past the side of the Methodist chapel, notice the separate entrances for Boys and Girls, which led into the day school beneath the church.

At the top go through the gate, turn right and you find yourself in Goodridge country. As a young architect, Henry Goodridge was employed by William Beckford to build his tower on Lansdown, and to create various picturesque structures in the extensive grounds that led up to the Tower. This doubtless helped to establish a reputation for the young man and he was soon employed to build a new bridge, which you will see if you continue down towards the traffic lights and follow the road as it bends round to the right, past houses also designed by Goodridge as an approach to the bridge. Greek Revival was the fashionable style at this time (1827), and the toll houses are little gems, with sturdy Doric columns. The bridge itself was cast-iron, and still has fine ironwork balustrades. The houses have incised lines in the Greek manner, and some really beautiful iron balconies. Wreaths were a favourite motive of Goodridge's, and here they are, decorating houses on both sides of the road. Bridge and buildings all bear the name of the Duke of Cleveland, Lord of the Manor of Bathwick. The building nearest the bridge on the eastern side is later than the rest, being built in 1845 as a dispensary. These were private charities which gave medical treatment to the poor, and Bath had several. This one, as the plaque over the door tells you, owed its existence largely to the efforts of John Ellis, who died in 1856. Internally it keeps its arrangements of waiting and consulting rooms, although it is now an art gallery. It also took private patients; the little door to the right of the main door was their discreet entrance.

In the garden which runs down to the river on the downstream side of the bridge are said to be some relics of a John Wood building. Look over the wall, and you will see a complete Ionic column not far from the river's edge, and a bit of one by the house. It is thought that these come from Wood's church in Queen Square, built when he was refused permission to reconstruct St. Michael's, but pulled down about 1875 when the road was widened to allow access to the Midland Railway Station. The curse of traffic schemes had struck once again. One or two Victorian house owners seemed to have taken the opportunity to rescue bits of the church for their gardens. Looking back to the new development, you will also notice that it includes an old malthouse, the square building with the white ventilator at the top.

As you retrace your steps from the bridge, you look up towards Walcot Parade, which towers above a raised pavement. When built in the 1770s the houses were called Swithin's Terrace and Butler's Buildings, and had a fine, uninterrupted view of the river. Beyond them to the right and next to the road is a row called Anglo Terrace. It gets its name from the Anglo-German Brewery which stood behind it; the premises still survive and loom up behind the terrace. Walk back towards Walcot Street, but this time pass in front of *Walcot Chapel* and take a good look at the Rev. Jenkins' handiwork. He designed a similar building in Lambeth two years later. After the chapel comes a row of five shops, the last of which was once a butcher's. You can tell this by the wide eaves with the bars for hanging out the meat and poultry on show. An old law said that all shops had to have open fronts with all goods on display above the counter: in other words, to be open and above board. This shop is unusual in having retained its old security shutters, here converted into windows. At the front the slot and staple for the shutter bar are visible, and at the side the shutter bar is still in position. There was another pub on the other side of the alleyway, where now there is a furniture shop, and there is yet another just coming up, *The Hat and Feather*. Courts such as St. Swithin's Place were built over its old yard.

* Cross the road to the short flight of steps by *Walcot Parish Church*, turn left at the top and just before you reach the church itself, peer through the railings. Immediately in front of you is the gravestone of the Reverend George Austen, Jane's father. He was married in the old church and buried in the crypt of the new one, from where this stone has been removed to be put on show. The larger tomb, moved from its original home in the lower graveyard, is Fanny Burney's, although naturally it has her married name of d'Arblay. Though fluttery, gossipy, and at times downright spiteful, one cannot help but admire her physical courage. In an age when medicine was primitive, she had her first and only child when she was 42, and sixteen years later faced the nightmare of a mastectomy. It was, of course, without the benefit of anaesthetics. One's only hope was to faint with the pain. Yet Fanny recovered and lived to be 87.

Cross the road at the pedestrian crossing and you will see in front of you a steep flight of steps. To photograph the church you should climb up here until you reach the gate on the left, which leads into Hedgemead Park, where you will get the best view. (You will have to return the same way.) As you climb, you notice Gloster Villas on your right. These are all that remain of a mass of little streets, many of which began to come into existence shortly after Camden Crescent was built. In view of the fact that the crescent itself had to be left incomplete due to the instability of the ground, the folly of building here can only be described as staggering. In the late 1870s a series of slips began, which destroyed many of these little homes, and the 1886 OS map shows just odd buildings here and there; many of those were unsafe. The decision was taken in 1888 to pull them down and put the park in their place. So Mullin's Court, the raison d'être of the flight of steps, disappeared along with many others (including two more pubs). A pretty little bandstand, the earliest surviving in Bath, stands at the top of the park to commemorate its opening. The area was originally called Edgemead, and seems to have acquired the H due to mistaken gentrification.

Stand opposite the church and you will be able to see its front entrance, and next to it the Verger's House, built in a rather rustic style. Beyond that again is a wall, with what look like upside-down ice-cream cones carved on it. These are inverted torches, a classical symbol of death: the flame of life has been extinguished. Behind the wall are the catacombs. Wedged into the corner between the Paragon and Guinea

Lane is *The Star*, one of the most interesting pubs in Bath. It was first licensed about 1760, and at a later date was licensed to Daniel Aust, a cabinet-maker and builder. It is possible that he paid his workmen in the pub, so that the money quickly returned to his pockets. It was refitted in the 19th century by a company called Gaskell and Gaskell, and amazingly it still retains all these fittings. If you want to know what a Victorian pub looked like, visit *The Star*. Its original front door is in Guinea Lane, but before you climb, look across to No.33 The Paragon, now called *Siddons' House*. Sarah Siddons, the great tragedian, lived here from 1779 until she left the city in 1782 for London. Although she would earn much more in the capital, she was sorry to go, but at the final performance she told the audience she had three reasons for leaving – and brought her three children on stage. Reports indicate there was literally not a dry eye in the house. Her portraits show a woman not beautiful in a conventional way, but extremely striking. The bronze plaque was unveiled in 1922 by another great actress, Ellen Terry.

Walk up Guinea Lane until you are opposite some little 18th-century houses on the left-hand side. One was the home of William Cottell, Furniture Remover: he used the bressumer as a sign-board. Houses like this are now known as artisan houses and are very fashionable. Cross towards them and begin to walk back down the lane, watching out for a flight of steps on your right. As you face down the steps, you have on your left *Walcot Schools*, now used on Wednesdays as an antiques market. It was erected in 1840 and designed by James Wilson, a local architect responsible for several schools in the area. It served no less than 1,000 children: 400 infants in the lowest section, 300 boys in the centre, and 300 girls in the upper section, each having a separate entrance. It moved in 1904 to the site you have already seen in Walcot Street. On your right is the *Kingdom Hall*, once a Roman Catholic church. As you descend the steps to the street below, (with great care: they are slippery when wet), look to your right along the backs of the houses. No.20, with the bay, was quite a grand house. Now go out on to the raised pavement facing the north side of The Paragon and turn right.

The houses to your right have the name Vineyards engraved on them, but are usually called Harlequin Row, from the variety in their appearance. They prove that not all houses in Bath were of Bath stone. Some are stuccoed, the plaster then being grooved to give the semblance of stone. Underneath there is brick. Some houses still have their fire-marks, the proof that the house was insured against fire. This was necessary because by and large it was the insurance companies that provided the fire engines. It is not true that the firemen would not put out a fire if the house did not bear the company mark: the companies collaborated between themselves, and the mark let them know from which company they should claim. However, they sometimes had to recruit bystanders to pump the water, and these liked to be paid in beer. If sufficient was not forthcoming, they would stop, chanting "No Beer – No Water!" They usually got their way!

The next building of interest is set back from the rest, and is in the Gothick style. It is the chapel built for the Countess of Huntingdon, one of Wesley's first aristocratic converts. She took to Methodism with such enthusiasm that eventually she and Wesley fell out, since it became clear to him that she had every intention of being in charge. This chapel dates from 1765, and was enormously fashionable, though some, like Horace Walpole, went to mock. "I was glad to see that luxury was creeping in upon them before persecution," he wrote, accurately if maliciously, to a friend. It is now the home of the excellent Building of Bath Museum, which has a study centre. Next door to it is another delight, The Museum of British Folk Art. The paintings are certainly not great art; one art critic has been extremely dismissive of them, but has missed the reason for their charm. Real everyday people, often with real everyday animals, leap from the past in a way they do not from grander portraits. They are housed in what was the schoolroom for the chapel, built in 1842 to designs by Manners.

Vineyards, the official name for this row, refers to the fact that there was a vineyard on this site until the 18th century; according to some accounts it dated back to Roman times. Although this may seem surprising, wine is now grown extensively in Somerset on south-facing slopes like this. Just to the south of Bath is a combe called Vineyard Bottom. On old maps it usually appears as Whinyards. Still on the high pavement, walk along until Hay Hill, a paved lane, is on your right. Across the road is No.1 The Paragon, another building associated with the Austen family. Here lived the Leigh Perrots, Mrs Austen's brother and wife. Aunt Leigh Perrot was difficult to get along with, and Jane did not greatly care for her, but the family quickly united when her aunt was accused of theft (this story is told in 'Labyrinths and Lace'). One way and another, Bath was not a very happy place for Jane. It was no surprise that she left it with feelings of relief.

There is a ramp here leading from the high pavement; use it to cross the road. Walking westwards, you have on your left Bladud Buildings which some time about 1800 had a bow added, to the irritation of modern purists. It can be roughly dated by the bow windows having curved frames. The arrangement of the windows is also characteristic of this date. On the other side of the road is Fountain Buildings. The name is said to derive from a convent dating back to Saxon times, and dedicated to St. Werbergh. An oratory was placed in the church in 1170. By John Wood's day the church had become an alehouse, sited over the cistern which provided the water supply for the conduits on the northern side of the city. Wood calls it Werborough Church, and gives a different reason for its name. According to him, "we may conclude it to have been the Place of Sanctuary to which Murderers fled, and there paid their Fines for Murder: for such Fines were called Werae". So there you have it. The terrace itself dates principally from 1775, but contains *Fountain House* (out of sight from your position, a little way up Lansdown Road), which existed certainly as early as 1742.

With the advent of Broad Street on your left, the end of the walk is nearly in sight. On the far corner of the road is the *Royal York Hotel*. Originally it was a coaching inn, the *York House*, built by John Wood the Younger. It was grand enough for the then Princess Victoria to stay there when she visited the city in 1830, but at the time of writing it is in a state of decay. Turn left and walk down Broad Street. Watch out for the old entrance to the *YMCA* on the left, and a few yards below it you will discover a little alleyway. Now called Broad Street Place, it was once known as Gracious Street or Court, a name which can just faintly be seen on the southern wall. It was named after the builder, Gracious Stride, and truth to tell, it was a slum. It is shown in *The Sack of Bath* with the caption "Broad Street Place – Gone!" to which the only possible reply is "Thank Goodness". Even in the photograph it is possible to deduce that the houses were small, and by using the 1885/6 1:500 OS map one can work out that the ground floor of the biggest house was 11 foot by 11 foot, and the smallest about 8 foot by 11 foot. They were hovels: they may have been Palladian hovels, but they were still hovels, the word used by John Wood to describe some of the housing in the Walcot Street area. There were eight houses squeezed between the back of the shops and the steps which lead down to Walcot Street, with six more packed back to back to them on the north side. You can see the height by looking at what remains of the one at the rear of the shop. Another seven houses were arranged around the rest of the space. To save such properties would surely have been conservation carried to excess; instead we now have this pleasant open space, an oasis from the pollution of Broad Street itself. While the *YMCA* is not great architecture, it is fairly well hidden here, and serves a very useful purpose for young people. Gracious Stride, himself, by the way, did not live here, but in the more elegant surroundings of Gay Street. The wedges of ground between Milsom, Broad and Walcot Streets were filled with tiny courts like these; on the far side of Broad Street the entrances are now pedestrian ways into a car park; later, on the left-hand side below Saracen Street, you will notice that one or two shops have a doorway to each side, one of which would have led into the court at the back.

Take a deep breath of clean air before returning to Broad Street and crossing the road. The large Palladian building on the right, with the coat of arms, was King Edward's School, its home provided by the city after it had languished in the old church by the North Gate. It was not exactly an act of great generosity. When Edward VI set up the school, he gave large parts of the city to go with it, to provide the means of support for his free Grammar School. Unfortunately he appointed the Council as trustees. Bit by bit the Council (members of whom were involved in land development) appropriated the land, leaving the school in a parlous state. This is the reason why the city owns so much land today. Eventually, in 1711, the then master took the Council to court, and slowly change took place. Finally, in 1752 this building was begun on the site of an inn, *The Black Swan*. Traffic and its attendant pollution drove the school out in the late 1980s, but fate give it the last laugh. The building was sold for a substantial sum to be developed as offices, but the market then collapsed and recession set in. It has since been sold on at a loss. The junior school boys have now joined the senior school in pleasanter surroundings on the east side of the city.

Next to the school is the entrance to Shire's Yard, once a stable yard associated with Wiltshire, the carrier employed by Gainsborough. He did not charge the artist, saying it was an honour to be associated with his paintings. He even gave the artist a horse, when asked to lend one as a model. Gainsborough repaid his kindness by painting his portrait. The yard has now been turned into a shopping precinct, described in the guidebook by that dangerous word "tasteful".

At No.8 is the Postal Museum, an apt home for it, since it was the Post Office from 1821 until 1854. It was from here that the first letter with a stamp (the penny black) was sent, 2 days early. One wonders why someone was so anxious to be first, since the *Guinness Book of Records* had not yet been invented. Bath has many connections with the postal service, as this museum proves. Next door, at No.7, is a house within a house. It is usually said that the street derives its name from being the home of the broadloom weavers, which it certainly was. John Wood reckons there were about 60 in the one street. *St. Michael's Church* kept dying pots in the vestry for their use, and at the back, where Milsom Street now stands, is where the cloth, having been woven, dyed, and washed, was dried. The racks were called tenters, and to keep the cloth taut, it was hooked on. It was, in fact, on tenterhooks. However, Wood also insists it was a broad street. No.7 confirms this. The present frontage is 18th-century, but hidden away inside, and only visible inside the shop, is a house with the date 1640 and the initials MB. These stand for Mary Barber, who leased it at that time. (One is constantly surprised at how active women were in business in the 17th and 18th centuries.) Its position bears out Wood's estimate of the street being 35 feet wide. Many of the buildings are considerably older than the frontage indicates, and this can be seen by walking up the alleyway to *The Moon and Sixpence*; keep turning left until you are looking up the fire escape of a shop in Broad Street. Here you can see the original timber construction.

The age of these houses and shops, pre-dating true Palladian architecture, gives this end of the street a pleasing variety, especially the group just behind the church. No.38, opposite the Postal Museum, is the oldest, being built in 1709, but *The Saracen's Head* is not much younger. It claims to be Bath's oldest pub, and certainly goes back to 1713. It is the only survivor of the many Broad Street pubs; a hundred years ago there were six. One of its claims to fame is that Charles Dickens stayed there, but it was important long before that, for it appears on town maps from 1779 onwards, as one of the principal inns.

This is the end of this short but intensive walk, and after your efforts you may feel it necessary to investigate the inn further, or return to *The Podium*, to visit its restaurants on the first floor.

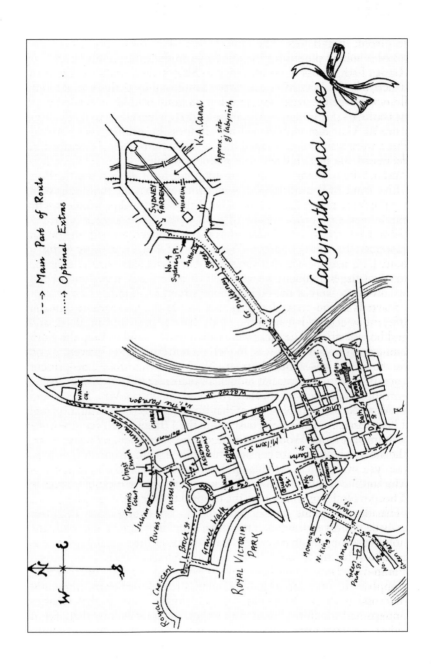

Labyrinths and Lace

Labyrinths and Lace

It is ironic that the city with which Jane Austen is so often connected in people's minds should be the place she most disliked. That city is, of course, Bath. It was the centre of the snobbery and artificial behaviour which was the butt of her humour, but in addition there were some unhappy family events which took place here, including the death of her father, which added to her distaste for the place. Her final departure from Bath she regarded with "happy feelings of Escape!" Nevertheless, there were also cheerful days, and the labyrinths and lace of the title represent the ups and downs, the happiness and the sorrow, of Jane Austen's life in Bath.

Like some of the other walks, this has an inner walk, with extensions for the more energetic. Unlike the others, even if you decide to cut out the longer bits, you should still read the paragraphs associated with them. Jane would undoubtedly have covered the whole distance, for she described herself as "a desperate walker". She thought nothing of taking quite long walks in the countryside; not only did she visit nearly all the nearby villages, frequently going across fields to reach them, but she also speaks of strolling by the canal, still a pleasant experience today.

Start: We begin in Abbey Church Yard, the centre of the fashionable life Jane so despised. It is considerably altered from her time. The shops and houses which clung to the sides of the *Abbey* have gone, and more pinnacles have arrived on the church itself. The shops which were next to the *Pump Room*, including what was once Gainsborough's house, have disappeared, replaced by the Concert Room, now used as the entrance to the *Roman Baths*. She would, however, recognise the *Pump Room* itself, built mainly by Thomas Baldwin between about 1784 and 1791. *Northanger Abbey*, the first of the Bath books, mentions the list of visitors kept in the room, and the parading which went on there during the morning, "looking at everybody and speaking to no-one" if you had not yet made an entrée into society. It was here that Catherine Morland, the unsophisticated heroine, first meets the fickle Isabella Thorpe. Noticing what she describes as "two odious young men", she persuades Catherine to watch them, until they leave, at which point Isabella desires to leave as well. She is not following them – of course not; it just happens that her route is the same as theirs. It is still possible to follow that route today. "Half a minute conducted them through the Pump-Yard to the archway, opposite Union Passage; but here they were stopped. Everyone acquainted with Bath may remember the difficulties of crossing Cheap Street at this point; it is indeed a street of so impertinent a nature, ... that a day never passes in which parties of ladies, however important their business, ... are not detained on one side or other by carriages, horsemen, or carts." With your back to the *Pump Room* you will see what Jane calls an archway, which does indeed bring you to Cheap Street. Almost opposite is Union Passage,

35

originally called Cock Lane. John Wood insists that this was a vulgar version of Locks Lane. 19th-century taste agreed and it was changed. Cheap Street is still busy, but the road surface and driving standards seem to have improved since Catherine and Isabella "were prevented crossing by the approach of a gig, driven along on bad pavement by a most knowing-looking coachman, with all the vehemence that could most fitly endanger the lives of himself, his companion, and his horse". Were you to follow in the footsteps of the two odious young men, and continue up Union Passage, you would be avoiding the yard of *The Bear Inn*, for Union Street itself did not exist until 1807. However, we shall leave the upper town until later, and make our way to Terrace Walk by taking the gap between the *Abbey* and the *Concert Room*, and turning left along York Street.

The large open space is where the Lower Rooms stood until they were burnt down in 1820. They were then replaced by the Bath Royal Literary and Scientific Institute, which in turn was demolished in 1933. Jane Austen might have been amused that such a serious establishment replaced what in her youth was a focal point of frivolity. There is a striking difference between *Northanger Abbey* and *Persuasion* in that the first describes Bath when it is still the place to be, socially. However, high society had already abandoned it, preferring the delights of Brighton. This caused a marked decline, and *Persuasion* shows a city that is the home of retired army and naval officers and a cheap resort for impoverished nobility such as Sir Walter Elliot, the father of her heroine Anne. Those who did come tended to avoid the Rooms except for concerts, and had private parties instead. But in *Northanger Abbey* the rooms are still crowded, and still presided over by a Master of Ceremonies. At the Lower Rooms, Catherine Morland is introduced to Henry Tilney. He is the perfect hero, light-hearted and witty, but kind and understanding. As the second son of General Tilney, he takes up the occupation so often decreed for second sons, that of a clergyman. David Cecil, in his *Portrait of Jane Austen*, suggests that perhaps she had Sydney Smith in mind when she created this character. She would certainly have known him; he was tutor to the Hicks Beach family, who were friends of the Austens. He was staying in Bath in the winter of 1797, the earliest definite date we have for Jane in Bath, and his sense of humour is very like that of Henry Tilney's.

Turn left along Terrace Walk and use the two pedestrian crossings to reach Parade Gardens, continuing northwards by the river. In the balustrade is a plaque commemorating the flood prevention scheme. Stand by it and face Pulteney Bridge. If you look up above the bridge, you will see a rather lop-sided crescent, with five columns under its central pediment (a feature that distresses purists enormously). This is the ill-fated Camden Crescent, which had to be abandoned before it was complete, due to landslips (see 'The Ups and Downs of Lansdown' and 'The Street of Strangers'). Despite its history, it was a highly fashionable place to live when Jane wrote *Persuasion* about 1815. So it is there that she places the snobbish Sir Walter Elliot in "a lofty dignified situation". The whole thing was doubtless meant to be symbolic – where everyone could see the Man of Fashion, even though his position was rather ramshackle. The house is described as the best in Camden Place (the original name) so it appears Jane imagined them in the central feature. It is described as a "toilsome walk" for Anne Elliot, and is not included in this tour! Instead, cross Pulteney Bridge and walk down to Laura Place, crossing the road by the chemist's shop. The Pulteney family had intended a great estate here, firstly planned by Robert Adam, who was responsible for the bridge, but it was Thomas Baldwin who produced the final plans. Bankruptcies and war caused a slump in building, and the great plan came almost to nothing. Just the first half of the central spine, Great Pulteney Street, came into existence, terminating at this end in this roughly octagonal space. It is here we find Viscountess Dalrymple and her daughter, the Honourable Miss Carteret, the very superior relations with whom Sir Walter Elliot is so keen to establish a connection. Jane's loathing of snobbery comes out nearly every time they make an appearance, and she can be very skilful at demolishing people, real or imagined, when she chooses: "… they were nothing. There was no superiority of manner, accomplishment, or understanding. Lady Dalrymple had acquired the name of 'a charming woman' because she had a smile and a civil answer for everybody. Miss Carteret, with still less to say, was so plain and so awkward, that she would never have been tolerated in Camden Place but for her birth." It was in Laura Place, or its vicinity, that Jane's father was hoping to find lodgings when in 1800 he and his wife made the decision to retire to Bath. "Well girls! It is all settled. We have decided to leave Steventon and go to Bath." Thus did Mrs. Austen break the news. So great was Jane's dislike of the city that she is reputed to have fainted with horror. As we shall see shortly, the family found a home not too far away, and it is thought that they probably attended *Laura Chapel*, a proprietary chapel whose entrance was in Henrietta Street. The Chapel collapsed (literally!) early this century, and the remains were swept away, though the entrances survive.

In May of 1801, Jane and her mother spent considerable time house-hunting in Bath, trying to find something pleasant *and* economical, while sister Cassandra and the Reverend Austen stayed at Steventon, selling up the old home. With their arrival, it seems that a firm decision could be reached, and a house was taken which had been advertised in the local paper nearly all the time that Jane and her mother had been in the city, without their considering it suitable. The following advertisement had appeared in the *Bath Chronicle* on 21st May 1801: "The lease of No.4 Sydney Place, 3 years and a quarter of which are unexpired at Midsummer. The situation is desirable, the Rent very low, and the Landlord is bound by Contract to paint the first two floors this summer. A premium will therefore be expected." Perhaps the Austens felt they simply could not go on looking at houses any longer, and decided to take this one, even though there was a premium. The house is at the far end of the street, so if you decide to keep to the inner walk, you should pick up the tour again at the paragraph marked #, but read the intervening paragraphs for information.

Walk the full length of Great Pulteney Street, veer left, cross Sutton Street, and you will find yourself in Sydney Place. No.4 has a plaque. Designed by Baldwin to face the pleasure gardens he was involved in developing (until bankruptcy overtook him), the terrace is pleasing without being ostentatious. They were here for three years before moving again, to Green Park Buildings. It was a happy choice for Jane, for it brought her conveniently close to one of her favourite bits of Bath, Sydney Gardens Vauxhall. The *Improved Bath Guide* of 1813 describes them as follows. "Sydney-Garden Vauxhall is at the extremity of Great Pulteney-Street and amply supplies the absence of other amusements during the summer months; it is an elegant specimen of the ability of Mr Masters, who laid out the ground, (about 16 acres.) Everything that taste and attention can effect to render this retreat agreeable to its visitors, may be found here; and perhaps no place in England of the same kind offers so many invitations as this to its pleasing shades."

"The amusements commence early in the spring with public breakfasts, promenades, and splendid illuminations, enlivened by music and every other fascination that labour and expense can provide. It is decorated with waterfalls, pavilions, and alcoves. The Kennet and Avon canal glides through this elysian scene, over which are two elegant cast-iron bridges after the manner of the Chinese. A sham castle planted with several pieces of cannon, bowling greens, swings, a labyrinth formed by enclosed path-ways, the principal one of which, after many intricate windings, leads to a fine Merlin swing and a grotto of antique appearance." It goes on to describe the ride that surrounded the gardens "free from dust in the summer and dirt in the winter" (it had been 'Mac-Adamized') and the hotel at the entrance "where families of distinction may be well accommodated". Did they turn away those that were not sufficiently distinguished, one wonders? At that time, if you did not have a season ticket, it was 6d. to go in. One should also note that this confirms that Bath was really a winter resort, with only the gardens providing entertainment in summer. The labyrinth disappeared when the railway came through, but the grotto may be the one in the grounds of the Bath Spa Hotel. (There is evidence both for and against this theory.)

Walk to the end of Sydney Place, cross the road, and wander for a time in the gardens, as Jane herself did so often. In 1799, she wrote to Cassandra, her sister, to tell her that there was to be "a grand gala on tuesday evening in Sydney Gardens: a Concert with Illuminations & fireworks" but she wrote again nearly three weeks later to say "Last night we were in Sidney Gardens again, as there was a repetition of the Gala which went off so ill on the 4th. – We did not go until nine, & were in very good time for the Fire-works, which were really beautiful

38

Sydney Gardens in Jane Austen's Day. From a print by Nattes, 1806

and passing my expectation. The weather was as favourable as it was otherwise a fortnight ago." The weather was not the only problem for organisers of pyrotechnic events. In 1813, there was to have been a really stupendous display, and it was advertised that, amongst other wonders, "Phaeton will descend in a fiery car, whose wheels, in rapid rotation, will set the world on fire; and the whole garden will appear in one mighty blaze!" Unfortunately the wheels did not rotate, and the world was not set on fire – instead the whole apparatus collapsed, to the dissatisfaction of the crowd. It seems that someone had climbed into the trees and tampered with the workings. In 1804, there was an event which Jane might have attended, for the Bath Harmonic Society held a Grand Fête Champêtre at which not less then 1700 persons sat down to an elegant breakfast. There was a firework display and other amusements, which over 4,000 people attended. Today the gardens have declined, and although they are a peaceful park there are no remains of the many attractions, such as the Hermit's Cot, the Miller's Habitation, and in 1830, a fountain displaying various Hydraulic experiments. Since Jane herself was in hope that the Concert would have more than its usual charm for her "as the gardens are large enough for me to get pretty well beyond the reach of its sound" it is possible she would prefer the present, quieter grounds. Make your way out to the southern arm of Sydney Place, and return to Great Pulteney Street, which is to the right. You may wish to visit the Holburne of Menstrie Museum or its tea-house first. Both are closed from December to March.

Return up this wide street where Jane Austen places Catherine Morland's lodgings, and Lady Russell, Anne Elliot's friend, is looking for "drawing-room window-curtains ... described as the handsomest and best hung of any in Bath". It is an odd thing to be looking for, and indeed she is simply avoiding mention of Captain Wentworth, who had been standing in the street, for it had been she who had persuaded Anne that she should not marry him (one of the acts of persuasion from which the title comes).

Return over Pulteney Bridge, cross by the Art Gallery and walk up to the High Street, turning left to stand near the entrance to the market. We must remember that this corner of Bath is completely changed from Jane's day. The wings to the *Guildhall* are creations of the late 19th century. Instead, there were inns lining the High Street, of which just *The Christopher* remains. Until the 1770s the old market hall stood out in the centre of the street by the *Abbey*, and even in the 19th century, this was known as The Market Place. The markets themselves were to the back and on each side of the *Guildhall*. The *Improved Bath Guide* describes them as excelling "all others of the same extent in the kingdom ... Here may be found a good supply of fish, flesh, and fowl, and every other kind of provision at moderate prices; fresh butter, equal to any in England, is brought from the country every morning; and the butchers who live in the city supply the inhabitants with the best of meat every day of the week." Jane confirms this in a letter to Cassandra in 1801, though she is worried about the price of fish: "I am not without hopes of tempting Mrs Lloyd to settle in Bath; meat is only 8d. per pound, butter 12d., and cheese 9½d. You must carefully conceal from her, however, the exorbitant price of fish: a salmon has been sold at 2s. 9d. per pound the whole fish." She adds, with a typical piece of Janeite cynicism, that she thinks the price will go down when the Duchess of York leaves the city.

Leave the market behind you, cross the road, turn right, and then left along Upper Borough Walls. As you pass along here, you will notice on your left the top of Union Passage, made almost redundant by the 19th-century Union Street (vying in elegance and uniformity with Milsom Street, as our 1813 guidebook has it). Before its creation, the busy stable yard of *The Bear Inn* separated the old town from the new. It was doubtless *The Bear* that Jane had in mind when she refers in *Persuasion* to the principal inn of the city. As with many others, mail and stage coaches for various parts of the country would have set off from here, though the less glamorous inns were the departure points for the distinctly down-market carts and waggons. Readers of Thomas Hardy's *The Trumpet Major* will recall Bob's disappointment when his intended bride turns up on the Sunday waggon although he had given her money to arrive in style on the Royal Mail coach. One coach route to Bath from London was via Devizes, a route with which Jane was familiar. It came past Lacock Abbey, and although it is in Wiltshire and not Gloucestershire, where she places her fictional Northanger Abbey, it resembles closely the latter's description, being low-lying with a level gravel drive, and with wooded hills behind it. It *was* a convent, and there *are* traces of the cloister. Returning to Bath, Union Street is mentioned in *Persuasion*, for although it was not completed until Jane had left the city, she kept her information up to date.

Running parallel with Upper Borough Walls is New Bond Street, built as a carriage road in 1806, and replacing the old Frog Lane (definitely not an elegant name). Jane refers only to Bond Street, however. Continue a little further along Upper Borough Walls, cross to your right, and you will find it, now called Old Bond Street. Or rather, you will find part of it. It was originally two blocks long, but only the southern block remains. The other disappeared in 1810 and the corner of Quiet Street altered to make it easier for traffic to turn into Milsom Street. One shudders to think what the conservation lobby would make of such a suggestion now! It is in Bond Street that Sir Walter Elliot stood in a shop and counted 87 women go by without there being a tolerable face among them, and where Catherine Morland finds one of the Miss Thorpes loitering towards Edgar Buildings, where the Thorpes had their lodgings. Edgar Buildings can be seen at the top end of Milsom Street, with the pediment which gives a focal point as you walk up towards it. Until the Victorian builders raised the roof-lines on the banks at the far end of Milsom Street, the roof-lines met those of Edgar Buildings, giving a pleasing perspective to the street. It was built as a street of houses in the 1760s but shops and banks are quick to recognise a good site, and they began to move in. Thus in both Bath books it is where the characters go shopping. Here Isabella Thorpe sees "the prettiest hat" and Admiral Croft finds a print shop which contains the seascape which he finds ridiculous. "What queer fellows your fine painters must be, to think that anybody would venture their lives in such a shapeless old cockleshell as that!" he exclaims to Anne Elliot. With two brothers in the Royal Navy, Jane must have been familiar with comments like this. Yet this was still a good address for lodgings: Jane puts the Tilney family in Milsom Street. Walk up to Milsom Street by crossing Quiet Street. The second shop up was Molland's, the pastry cook's, which occurs in *Persuasion*. The scene is, in some ways, a turning point in the book, but it gives Jane a chance to take another quick dig at Bath, this time its weather. "I have equipped myself properly for Bath, you see," says Captain Wentworth, and indicates his new umbrella. Although the shop has acquired a certain fame through its inclusion in the novel, not everyone was enamoured of it. In 1810, the Council was required "to consider a letter from Mr. Henry Crook complaining of the dangerous state of his house in Milsom Street in this city occasioned by an oven and flue in Mrs. Molland's house adjoining and to resolve thereon". The Council ducked the issue by saying that Mr. Crook should have applied to Mrs. Molland first, which he had failed to do, and they therefore deferred it. His complaint does not appear again, so one must assume it was settled amicably.

As you continue up Milsom Street, look above the shop fronts on the right-hand side and you will notice an advertisement for a circulating library and reading room, not to mention the state lottery if a little gentle betting was desired. Although dated at about 1820, it is redolent of the period of which Jane is writing. Cross the road to the National Westminster Bank, which lives in Somerset Buildings, a Baldwin confection of the 1780s, built on the site of the old Poor House. It became a bank within ten years of its erection, but the beautiful ceiling in the banking hall gives some idea of the interior of the wealthier houses in this street. At the top of Milsom Street, turn right, cross Broad Street, walk past Bladud Buildings and stop outside No.1 The Paragon, nearly opposite *Hay Hill House*. At the time of writing this has a dejected appearance, but in the 1790s it was the winter home of those pillars of respectability, Mr. and Mrs. James Leigh Perrot, Jane's uncle and aunt. He seems to have been a kindly and amusing man, and there are frequent references to him in the letters to Cassandra, but Aunt Leigh Perrot was more difficult. Though Jane is cautious in her comments, we get the picture of a rather severe, dominant woman, easily offended. There is a reference to a coolness between her aunt and a Mrs. Bond, which Jane describes as "the oddest kind of quarrel in the world" with just a hint that it is her aunt who is keeping the distance, for her uncle and Mrs. Bond were on civil terms. Yet despite this, there were strong family ties which came to the fore when Mrs. Leigh Perrot was accused of shop-lifting shortly after Jane's visit to Bath in 1799. This story will be told outside the shop where the incident occurred. Her aunt was, in happier times, in the thick of the social whirl which her niece so disliked, and in this house there were many of those private parties which Jane found stupid: "perhaps if larger they might be less intolerable, … Ly Fust, Mrs. Busby & a Mrs. Owen sat down with my Uncle to Whist within five minutes after the three old *Toughs* came in, and there they sat … till their chairs were announced. – I cannot anyhow continue to find people agreeable."

We leave the Leigh Perrots and continue along The Paragon. On the left-hand side you will soon see *The Countess of Huntingdon's Chapel*, (see 'The Street of Strangers' for its history). The Countess died in 1796, but Jane would certainly have known about her and, playing the speculation game, one wonders if she lives on as the autocratic Lady Catherine de Burgh, in *Pride and Prejudice*. She too liked to have a clergyman under her wing who would preach her brand of Christianity. We are on safer ground when we eventually reach *Walcot Parish Church*. (Here again its history is detailed in 'The Street of Strangers'.) It was in the old church that George Austen and Cassandra Leigh were married, in 1764. He was unusually good-looking, intelligent, and by no means badly off, while his wife was vivacious, witty, and with numerous aristocratic relations. Despite this, she took naturally to life in the Rectory at Steventon, their Hampshire home. It was in this gifted, happy atmosphere that the Austen children were raised; it is no wonder that Jane was so sad to leave it, when her father sought retirement here in 1801. Bath was his home for less than four years, before he died in January 1805 of what Jane calls a feverish complaint. He was buried in the crypt of the new church, from where the stone has been removed to be seen in the grassy area to the east of the church. The other monument is that of Fanny Burney, a writer Jane admired.

Somewhere near the church, possibly in Walcot Street itself, was a cheap shop selling hat decorations. We know this, for Jane writes at length on the subject to Cassandra in 1799. "Flowers are very much worn, & Fruit is more the thing. Eliz: has a bunch of Strawberries, & I have seen Grapes Cherries, Plumbs & Apricots – There are likewise Almonds & raisins, french plumbs & Tamarinds at the Grocers, But I have never seem any of them in hats, – A plumb or greengage would cost about three shillings; – Cherries & grapes about 5 I beleive – but this is at some of the dearest shops;– My aunt has told me of a very cheap one near Walcot Church, to which I shall go in quest of something for you." In the next letter she says she has been to the

shop "and very cheap we found it, but there are only flowers made there, no fruit". Always economical, she opts for the flowers since she can get so much more for her money, and "Besides, I cannot help thinking that it is more natural to have flowers grow out of the head than fruit. What do you think on that subject?" Her letters are full of light-hearted chat about fashion including a little drawing of the back of a dress: Jane was certainly not a frump, and she delighted in looking smart. "I saw some gauzes in a shop in Bath Street yesterday at only 4s. a yard, but they were not so good or so pretty as mine", she says proudly.

Cross the road at the pedestrian crossing, turn left, and climb Guinea Lane branching off to the right. At the top, cross Lansdown Road (with great care – it is not a pedestrian-friendly street). Before walking down Julian Road, turn back and look across Lansdown Road to the raised pavement just to your right, which is what in *Persuasion* is called "the greater space and quiet of Belmont". You will doubtless be glad to hear that this is as high as you will climb, so spare a thought for the sedan chairmen, who carried people around the city, even up the steepest streets. No-one thinks anything of suggesting that Anne Elliot should take a chair from the centre of town to Camden Crescent, a hefty climb for the chairmen up Lansdown Hill. What is more, the ground was not deemed officially hilly (when they could charge an increased fare) until they reached this crossroads. It was not, however, a cheap form of transport. (For more information see 'A Transport of Delight'.)

Now turn and walk along Julian Road. Its original name was Cottle's Lane, and like many 18th-century streets, its individual terraces had names too. This side was called Montpelier, and by continuing along it, you will reach *Christ Church*. Just beyond it, where there is a building which has been church, church hall and now homes, was a riding school. To the north is a museum, housed in what was once a Royal or Real Tennis Court. Stables and court are advertised in The *Improved Guide* of 1813. "Ladies and gentlemen may here amuse themselves every morning with this agreeable exercise. An experienced riding-master constantly attends from nine till two o'clock, for the purpose of instructing them in the polite art of riding gracefully, and properly managing their horses." The tennis court was "extremely commodious, and respectably attended by lovers of athletic sport". It was probably this riding school that Jane had in mind when she wrote rather sadly to Cassandra after their father's death; "This morning we have been to see Miss Chamberlayne look hot on horseback. – Seven years & four months ago we went to the same Ridinghouse to see Miss Lefroy's performance! – ... But seven years I suppose are enough to change every pore of one's skin, & every feeling of one's mind." The joyous tone of her early letters is never quite recaptured after the loss of her father. Cross the road opposite the church, and turn right along Rivers Street. This was another fashionable address, so much so that Lady Russell, Anne's friend and mentor, has her lodgings there. This may be due partly to an association of ideas in her creator's mind, for the street immediately on the left is Russel Street. It proved rather too expensive for Fanny Burney when she retired here with her emigré husband, Count d'Arblay, and they had to move. Now take Russel Street, and go down to the *Assembly Rooms*. Provided the Rooms are not being used, you can walk round them free of charge, although you are advised to check at the entrance. There is a charge for visiting the Museum of Costume.

These rooms were opened in 1771, and are the only ones to survive, something they have achieved only by the skin of their teeth (if rooms can be allowed teeth). There can be no greater indication of the change in Bath between the writing of the two Bath books than the scenes at the *Assembly Rooms* (or Upper Rooms, as Jane rightly distinguishes them). In *Northanger Abbey*, Catherine Morland is late in arriving and the rooms are very crowded. She can see nothing of the dance but "the high feathers of some of the ladies". It is only towards the end of the evening, when the dancing is over, that there is room to walk about in comfort. A French account dating from this period says the onlookers were held back by men with wooden bars to allow room for dancing. By the time of *Persuasion*, the theatre and rooms "were not fashionable enough for the Elliots, whose evening amusements were solely in the elegant stupidity of private parties". Beau Nash, in Bath's heyday, had forbidden these private parties, because he could see they detracted from the social events, and encouraged snobbery. Without him, they gradually returned, and by the start of the 19th century the effect was as Jane noted in 1801: "Before tea, it was rather a dull affair; but then the tea did not last long, for there was only one dance, danced by four couple. – Think of four couple, surrounded by about an hundred people, dancing in the upper Rooms at Bath! – After tea we *cheered up*; the breaking up of private parties sent some scores to the Ball, & tho' it was shockingly and inhumanly thin for this place, there were enough I suppose to have made five or six very pretty Basingstoke assemblies." However, the rooms were well attended when someone such as Lady Dalrymple arranged a concert on behalf of a protégé. The Elliots arrive early and take their station by one of the fires in the Octagon Room.

On entering you find a wide corridor leading to the Little Octagon, with an entrance to the Ballroom on the left, and a door to the Tea Room on the right. Straight ahead is the Great Octagon, which was originally designed as the card room. Although gambling for high stakes had been made illegal in 1745, so that if you lost more than £10, you could be punished, within that restriction card-playing was still legal. It was so fashionable that it was found necessary to add the Card-Room at the far end, just six years after the opening. It was in the Great Octagon that the party awaited the arrival of Lady Dalrymple; the concert itself was probably in the Tea Room. It was certainly used for that purpose in the 18th century, although it was, as its name implies, the place where visitors such as Catherine Morland had supper on Ball nights. Now leave the Rooms, and imagine that it is a fine afternoon during 1799. Catherine Morland, like Jane Austen herself, might well have whiled away the afternoon by walking to Royal Crescent, so let us do the same. Turn right out of the *Assembly Rooms*, left along Bennett Street, into the Circus, and out by the western exit. This takes us to Brock Street; continue along here and into Royal Crescent at the far end.

Catherine Morland was here, enjoying an afternoon promenade with the Thorpes and her brother, when she discovered that John Thorpe had cancelled her outing with the Tilneys. She ran after them in the direction from which you have come, going south out of the Circus to their lodgings in Milsom Street. The others had wanted her to come with them in a carriage ride to Blaise Castle, an 18th-century folly in Bristol. It is true that riding on horseback or in a carriage was an option for the afternoon, but parading, simply walking up and down the wide pavements, some of which were called the Parades, was a feature of the 18th-century day which persisted right through the period, and was fashionable in all European spas. Jane herself usually went in for lengthier walks, but she refers in 1799 to "Lady Willoughby" who "is to present the Colours to some Corps of Yeomanry or other, in the Crescent" and in May 1801 she walks in Crescent Fields, though the weather was too cold for her to stay long. The Crescent Fields stretched from the haha (the wall and ditch at the southern limit of Crescent Lawn) right down to what is now the A4, and was a farm. It was not until 1830 that the Park came into being. Beyond the Crescent, to the west, are Marlborough Buildings, erected about 1790. Here stayed the Wallis's, the friends of Anne Elliot's cousin Walter, "in very good style". Before leaving this spot, you may wish to visit the museum at No.1 Royal Crescent, to get the feeling of a house of the period.

Return to Brock Street and take the footpath on the right which leads to the Park. You will soon see another walk on your left, at the back of the gardens of the Brock Street houses. This is the Gravel Walk, and is the route you should take. Gravel Walk does not appear on the 1779 map of Bath, but it is clear it was all part of the Brock Street/Royal Crescent development, for in the agreement with the landowner Sir Benet Garrard, John Wood the Younger had free use of a footway for chairs and passengers from Queen Square, behind Gay Street, up to the Royal Crescent. This explains why the houses on the south side of Brock Street have a regular appearance at the back, unlike the usual 'Mary Ann' façades to the rear. It features most notably in *Persuasion*, when Anne Elliot and Captain Wentworth "decide their direction towards the comparatively quiet and retired gravel walk". There is a Bath joke here which must pass most readers by. The two are supposed to be on their way to Camden Place, but this route is the most enormous detour! However, they have a great deal to talk about, as Jane is at pains to stress. As you go down the Gravel Walk, look out on your left for the Georgian Garden, and if you are doing this walk between May and October, go in. The houses in which the Austen family stayed in Bath must have had just such gardens as this. At the end of the Gravel Walk, negotiate the steps, turn left to reach Gay Street, and look up towards the Circus. The exact spot where you are standing once had a house on it, and this is where Mrs. Austen considered living in 1801, because it had a lower rent. After George Austen's death, the girls and their mother moved to No.25 Gay Street, on the right-hand side above the junction with George Street. It is now a dental surgery, but retains enough of the internal features for one to be aware that it was a fairly small but pleasing house. However, this walk turns right down Gay Street, into Queen Square. "My Mother hankers after the Square dreadfully," wrote Jane to Cassandra, discussing the problems of house-hunting, and it is not surprising that she did for they had had a happy stay here at No.13 in 1799. Turn right along the top of the square, cross to the western side, and stand outside No.19. This gives you a good view of No.13, the end house of the southern range, with Beechen Cliff looming up behind it.

The square is very altered from Jane's day, with some enthusiastic Victorian tree-planting obscuring the outlook across it. By the early 19th century it was out of fashion. "Remember, papa, if we do go (to Bath), we must be in a good situation: none of your Queen Squares for us," the Musgrove girls admonish their father, in *Persuasion*. In 1799, however, Edward Knight (Jane's brother but adopted by a wealthy, childless couple) brought his family, together with his mother and sister Jane to Bath, principally for his health, though both he and his mother seem to have been hypochondriacs. Jane wrote: "We are exceedingly pleased with the house; the rooms are quite as large as we expected. Mrs. Bromley is a fat woman in mourning, and a little black kitten runs about the staircase ... it is settled for us to be above, where we have two very nice-sized rooms," and adds, rather puzzlingly "with dirty quilts and everything comfortable." R.W.Chapman, who collected and edited the letters in 1932, suggests "dirty" may be a misreading of "dimity" which makes sense, for it was a stout cotton cloth often used for soft furnishings in the 18th century. From the drawing-room window Jane could see "the left side of Brock Street, broken by three Lombardy poplars in the garden of the last house in Queen's Parade". At the back, of course, was Beechen Cliff "that noble hill whose beautiful verdure and hanging coppice render it so striking an object from almost every opening in Bath". Walk down to the south-west corner, where you have a choice. If you are a Jane enthusiast, you will want to visit her home at Green Park Buildings, and you should follow the instructions in the next paragraph. If you do not feel up to this, why not sit in the gardens in Queen Square while you read the paragraph, then leave the square by Barton Street, in the south-east corner, walk down to the corner of Barton Street and Beauford Square, and turn into the square, picking up at the paragraph marked *.

If you decide to take the Green Park option, you should be warned that very little remains of the Bath that Jane Austen knew in this part of the town. Some of this was due to enemy action, but the vast bulk of the destruction was caused by modern developments. Nevertheless, it was in this part of Bath that the Austens pursued their house-hunting, so it is of interest. Walk down the right-hand side of Chapel Row, named after the John Wood church which stood in this corner. It was swept away to create a road to the Midland Railway Station. This will bring you to a crossroads: go straight across by *Holy Trinity Church* and continue to walk in a southerly direction down Charles Street. You will see on your right a street called New King Street, now blocked to vehicular traffic. Jane wrote: "I was glad to hear the former (her uncle) talk of all the houses in New King Street as too small; it was my own idea of them." She would be astonished to know that today some of them are divided into flats. She preferred Charles Street: "the buildings are new, and its nearness to Kingsmead Field would be a pleasant circumstance." Today it is defaced by the telephone exchange and *Kingsmead House* to your left, structures of such unsurpassable ugliness that it is hardly credible that anyone could seriously have sat down and designed them. Continue down to the traffic lights, where you see all that remains of Seymour Street, about which Jane was dubious. The houses have been replaced on one side by the *Salvation Army Citadel*, and on your side of the road by *Green Park Station*. This is at least an imposing building, even if it no longer serves its original purpose.

Walk in front of the station and cross the road on the far side. On your right you will see the surviving terrace of Green Park Buildings going off at an angle. There was once a similar terrace where now the modern old people's home stands, beyond the Salvation Army headquarters. The whole thing was rather a curious composition of the early 19th century, the two arms forming a V, with Seymour Street leading out of the apex of the V. It is not certain which architects and builders were involved, and the terrace you are looking at has a rather uneven appearance. Jane was suspicious of these houses because of the damp "of which there were symptoms," she remarks, darkly. She even goes so far as to call them "putrifying" in one letter. It is therefore surprising that when the lease ran out on Sydney Place they should have moved there, to No.27. Perhaps the rest of the family liked the interior, as Jane herself had. They should have listened to her doubts, and the complaints of other "discontented families". They had been there less than three months when Mr. Austen went down with a fever, and was dead within 48 hours. To add to Jane's distress, having written a letter to her brother Frank, they heard his ship had left Dungeness and was at Portsmouth, so she had to sit down and write it out all over again. The girls and their mother were now left in rather straitened circumstances, but the sons rallied round to assist. They saw out the lease of three months at Green Park before moving to Gay Street. Eventually Edward set them up in the house with which Jane is most associated, at Chawton. How happy Jane must have been to return to Hampshire! Walk back past the station, across at the lights to *Kingsmead House*, turn left, right, left at *The Griffin Inn*, and then right into Beauford Square.

* You are standing at the side of the *Theatre Royal*, built in 1805 to replace the old one in Orchard Street. This was the front entrance, but the whole interior was re-jigged after the fire in 1862. It was to the Orchard Street Theatre that Catherine Morland would have gone, and it was there that Sarah Siddons, the great tragedian, made her reputation. The play *Lovers' Vows* by Kotzebue was also produced here on several occasions during Jane's residence in the city. Although there is no record of her having seen it, she uses it in crucial scenes in *Mansfield Park*. The Austens themselves were enthusiasts for private theatricals, using an old barn at Steventon Rectory. However, since Jane seems to have kept up to date with changes in the city, we must assume that it was at this new theatre that Charles Musgrove obtained a box for his family. As you walk eastwards to the junction with Barton

Street, you will notice ahead of you a little street with a modern building on one side, and an old chapel used as a night-club on the other. This is Trim Street. Its most famous residents were the Wolfe family, but it was the last home of Mrs. Austen and her daughters in Bath. Their situation had changed from the days when Mrs. Austen could assure Cassandra "she will do everything in her power to avoid Trim Street, although you have not expressed the fearful presentiment of it which we rather expected".

Turn right past the present front of the *Theatre Royal*, and keep straight on, even when the pavement crosses between two roads. The buildings on the other side of the road are Westgate Buildings, although only a little section at the far end remains of the 18th-century terrace. This is where Anne Elliot's friend Mrs. Smith was in lodgings "in a very humble way". So humble was her home that Sir Walter Elliot remarks disdainfully, "Westgate Buildings must have been rather surprised by the appearance of a carriage drawn up near its pavement". Mrs. Smith was crippled with rheumatic fever, and was in a house with "a noisy parlour and a dark bedroom behind, and she never quitted the house but to be conveyed into the warm bath". She did not have far to go. Face the last house in the old part of Westgate Buildings, turn around, and you should have a garden in front of you, with a passageway on each side of it. Take the passage to the right of the garden, with an old, gabled building on your right. This will bring you to the *Hot* and *Cross Baths*, the latter to your left, and the other slightly to your right, across the road.

The *Cross Bath* is the coolest of Bath's three springs, so one can imagine that it was here that Mrs. Smith came. However, Edward Austen Knight himself came, perhaps to the *Hot Bath* itself and definitely to its *Pump Room*. The entrance to this was beneath the portico to the right, where the remains of a doorway can be clearly seen. At one time this was run by a gentleman called Hetling. On 2nd June 1799, Jane wrote: "He (Edward) drinks at the Hetling Pump, is to bathe tomorrow, and try Electricity on Tuesday." The name can still be seen on the wall facing the bath. From the baths, walk up the colonnaded Bath Street, and stand by the wall of the Pump Room (buskers or street entertainers permitting) looking across the street. To your right was *The White Hart*, one of the principal inns. It was demolished in 1867, and its sign is over the pub of the same name at Widcombe. Not only was Pickwick supposed to have stayed there, in Dickens' most cheerful novel, but the Musgrove family use it when they follow the Elliots to Bath. From the window Mary Musgrove saw the treacherous Mrs. Clay turn into Bath Street to meet Mr. Elliot. At the end of *Northanger Abbey* Jane links it with two similarly unpleasant characters, Isabella Thorpe and Captain Tilney. Maggie Lane, in her book about Jane in Bath, *A Charming Place*, suggests that this is no coincidence, for the street had unhappy connections for the Austen family. It was in a shop in Bath Street, perhaps the very shop where Jane

The King's Pump in the Pump Room, 1788. This was in the previous Room, but gives an idea of how the waters were served

saw the gauzes, that the incident occurred which resulted in Mrs. Leigh Perrot being accused of theft. The shop was one of those in the far quadrant forming the entrance of the street. The whole episode is quite odd, and is sometimes regarded by left-wing historians as yet another example of the Establishment grinding the working classes in the dirt. The facts seem to indicate something rather different, however.

Briefly, the story is that Mrs. Leigh Perrot bought some black lace in a shop known as Mrs. Smith's but run since her death by her sister Miss Gregory. This was made up into a parcel, and the Leigh Perrots, having paid, left the shop and continued walking in town. When they passed the shop again, Miss Gregory came out and accused Mrs. Leigh Perrot of theft. When the parcel was unwrapped, white lace was also inside. It was returned with the comment that there had been an error, but the male shop assistant ran after the Leigh Perrots demanding their name and address which was given. Miss Gregory and her assistant then went to the *Guildhall* and swore out a charge of attempted larceny against Mrs. Leigh Perrot who was arrested. There was no bail for such a charge when stolen goods were found in the possession of the accused, so Jane's aunt found herself in Ilchester Gaol. The next assizes were in March 1800, hence she was there for eight months. The girls offered to stay with her, but she gracefully declined. Fortunately for her, she was lodged with the gaoler and his family. The case aroused enormous interest, some of it rather macabre, for the value of the lace meant that if found guilty, Mrs. Leigh Perrot could have been sentenced to transportation or even death. Journalism being as opportunist then as it is now, a pamphlet was published after the trial with all the details. Although the author is careful to avoid the word, it soon became apparent, when the witnesses were called, that Miss Gregory and her staff had a nice line in blackmail. Other ladies came forward to say that something similar had happened to them, and while no-one mentions the word 'money' it is implied that most people, less strong-minded than the Leigh Perrots, paid up rather than undergo the ordeal of gaol and a trial. Other points were raised. If guilty, Jane Leigh Perrot had behaved in an extraordinary way, making no effort to hurry home with her ill-gotten gains, or conceal her identity. How had she put the lace into the parcel the assistant himself had wrapped? The jury took less than a quarter of an hour to find her not guilty, after a trial lasting nearly seven hours. Yet if today there are those who still suspect her of being guilty, we can imagine the effect it must have had in the gossipy, snobbish Bath of 1799. It was really no wonder that even when the sun shone, Jane disliked it. "I think I see more distinctly through rain. The sun was got behind everything, and the appearance of the place … was all vapour, shadow, smoke, and confusion," she wrote on her arrival in 1801. There is confusion about Jane, for stewards in the *Abbey* are sometimes asked where, amongst all the other tombs, is her grave. The answer is, of course, not in *Bath Abbey* but Winchester Cathedral, in her beloved Hampshire.

You may wish to conclude by visiting the *Pump Room*, and even taking the waters, although tea and coffee are available.

The Ups and Downs of Lansdown

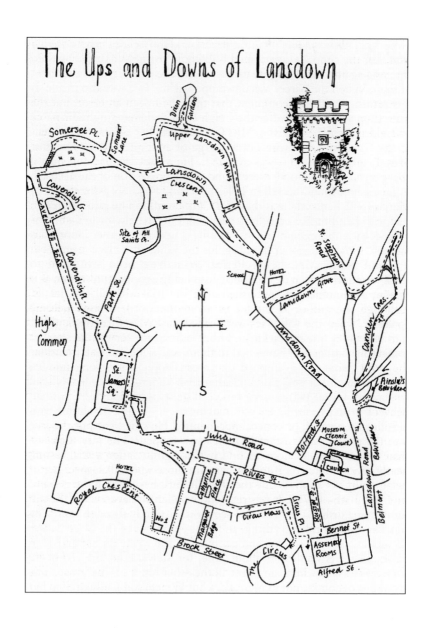

The Ups and Downs of Lansdown

This walk climbs above the Circus and the Royal Crescent to look at some of the other crescents and terraces which grace these northern slopes. En route, we shall find some Greeks, some elephants, and a disappearing post office.

Start: To make life simple, the walk begins in Bennett Street, beside the *Assembly Rooms*, a well-known Bath landmark, but we shall not stay there long, except to remark that these were opened in 1771, with a grand ball at which those who were in mourning were requested to lay it aside for the evening, so that the occasion would be colourful. Having allowed you to draw breath, we shall now begin climbing, and there is quite a lot of 'up' in this walk, to be matched with plenty of 'down' on the other side. Cross Bennett Street, climb Russel Street, go right and left around the end of Rivers Street, cross the next road, Julian Road, and stand outside *Christ Church*, completed in 1798. It was the first free church to be built in England since the Reformation as a result of concern for the poor who could not pay pew rent. The land was given by Lord Rivers, and has no parish because it was already in Walcot. The money was raised by voluntary subscription, and the seats on the ground floor were all free. There was a charge for a seat in the galleries, however, which were let out to "respectable families", and this gave a profit sufficient to defray the expenses. The architect was John Palmer, who built it in the fashionable Gothic revival style. An apse was added in 1886, which internally has some rather curious tiles, and the battlements were changed by Wallace Gill in 1900, but basically it remains much as Palmer left it. Some architectural experts take a dim view of it, which seems rather harsh.

Stand on the high pavement by the side of the church and look across at the entrance to Rivers Street. You will notice, if you look up at the roofs, that one of the houses, No.32, still has its original Cotswold stone tiles, as described in 'Windows and Things'. Slate was not used until the river was made navigable in 1727. Rivers Street is named after the family which ultimately owned much of this side of town. The road directly in front of you was Cottle's Lane until the Victorians discovered Roman remains. Having decided it was the Via Julia, they gave it its present name of Julian Road, although the Romans simply called it Highway 14. The address of *Christ Church* is properly Montpelier, the other side of the road being Brunswick Place, for a relic of 18th-century Bath are the streets within streets. Lansdown Road, for example, has Oxford Row, Belmont, and Belvedere, where we shall soon find ourselves. It must be a postman's nightmare! Turning clockwise until you have your back to the church, you are facing what is now used as dwellings but began life as a Roman Catholic chapel. The

Catholic congregation in Bath has had a very peripatetic existence, and at one time services were held at No.3 Brunswick Place, but this plot was purchased in 1851, at about the same time that *Christ Church* was expanding its grounds. It seems clear that the riding school which stood here, and is mentioned in 'Labyrinths and Lace', had declined at that time. The chapel, called St Mary's, had seating for 250, with standing room and galleries, which really is quite small, and in 1881 the congregation moved to a new church further along the street. The building then became the church hall for Christ Church before being converted to its present use.

Equestrianism was not the only form of recreation in this area. Turning clockwise again, and now facing north, you will see a museum called Mr. Bowler's Business. This was a Real or Royal Tennis Court, the game being a fore-runner of the modern game of squash, with very complicated rules. It was opened in 1777, and is described as being "respectably attended". It was built by Mr. Scrace, owner of the riding school, and the plans were said to have been given to him by the Earl of Pembroke and to be the same as the tennis court owned by the Duke of Orleans. By 1825 it had become the barley store for a brewery, and by the late 1960s was threatened with demolition. Fortunately a home was being sought for a unique collection of engineering equipment and mineral-water bottling machines, and today it is a fascinating museum of the industries associated with Bath, including Bath stone. There are special exhibitions from time to time, and as a result of one, a book was published called *Kegs and Ale*, on Bath pubs and breweries. It is from this that many details of local inns included in these walks come, confirmed, of course, by personal research. Little is left of the building's sporting past, but there are still numbers to be seen on an internal wall which were connected with the scoring.

Walk up towards the museum, but turn sharp right in front of the cottages dated 1856 so that you are at the back of the church. Here you find where economies were made during its erection. Just as you find rubble construction at the back of houses, you see it here too, although the windows still had to have tracery because they would be seen from inside. The arching in rubble-stone above them is to give strength. Now walk away from the church between the cottage and what is now an adult education centre, and you will find a footpath that climbs up at the back of the school into a little alleyway. There is nothing special about this alleyway, but it is certainly attractive. Its name was Nicholl's Court, now Nicholl's Place, and it brings you out to Belvedere, on Lansdown Road. Walk up the hill a little way, and on the other side of the road you will notice an archway, with arrows indicating Wellington Place and Wellington Terrace. Once upon a time this was true, but no longer. The original double-sided terrace called Wellington Place was badly affected in the landslips of the 1870s, and now all the houses have gone. You may walk down there, though you will have to retrace your steps. If you do, you must realise that where there are now gardens there were once 24 houses. Up the hill from the archway is a group of shops, one of which has an elaborate front with two carved heads. In its very recent history it has been a computer shop, DIY centre, and antiques shop, but the frontage including the shop window was put there in the 1870s by a Mr. Harding, who ran a chemist's. Eager to impress his customers with his erudition, he included the heads of two famous Greek medical men, Galen and Hippocrates, and through all the changes, they have remained. A little way above that is a double shop numbered 27A and 27B. On the wall of the building can faintly be seen an advertisement for a gentleman called Bosley, slater and plasterer. This helps to provide the answer to the question "Where is No.1 Ainslie's Belvedere?"

Using the steps down from the raised pavement outside No.20, cross the road to Ainslie's Belvedere, the row opposite and set back. Mr. Ainslie was the landowner, and the earliest houses were built about 1765, for an advertisement appeared in the *Bath Chronicle* in April of that year: "To be let – a convenient compleat finish'd house at Mr. Ainslie's Belvedere." The smaller houses are of later date. The terrace is numbered from 2 to 9, yet the rate-books show a No.1, and only one No.27 Belvedere. In the mid-19th century Mr Bosley was the rate-payer of the first house, but the postal directories indicate that this gradually became known as 1A Ainslie's Belvedere and at the same time, 27A Belvedere. One hopes it was a happier work place for Mr. Bosley and son than it had been for some in the early 19th century. It was then a manufactory for a shop in New Bond Street, run by Mesdames Smith and Jones, where hand embroidery and needlework could be purchased. An advertisement of 1817 describes it flatteringly as a place where "the friendless, the infirm, the unfortunate; and many who having seen better days turn to a source of pecuniary emolument those talents once cultivated as an elegant accomplishment". It goes on to decry machine needlework on the grounds that "Women and girls would be nearly excluded from almost the only employment nature and custom appear to have designed them for". This seems a bit rich coming from two business women with shops in Cheltenham and Bath. In fact it was probably a sweat shop. As early as 1825 a letter to the *Bath and Cheltenham Gazette* described this sort of occupation for women as "an unhealthy sedentary employment, to the destruction of their sight and constitution, for 16 and even 18 hours out of the 24".

No.8 is called *Gainsborough House* and has long been associated with the artist, which is puzzling, because there is absolutely no evidence to show that he ever lived there or had any connection with it. Indeed, at the time that he moved out of the centre of Bath, these houses had not even been built. It is now thought that he lived at *Lansdown Lodge*, a mid-18th-century house further up the hill, which unfortunately we do not pass on this route. It answers much more closely his description of it as a cottage, "sweetly situated". Until as late as 1835 No.9 was Walcot Police Station, and here prisoners could be tried, and confined in the cellar after conviction. Bringing us right up to date, No.2 Ainslie's Belvedere was the home of Roland Orzabal, one half of the pop group Tears for Fears. And with that let us leave these houses and continue up Lansdown Road, but not without noticing the shop on the corner, which until very recently was a butcher's shop. The wide eaves and rails for hanging meat and poultry indicate it must have been one for a very long time.

At the corner you will reach a complicated junction. This is clearly a thirsty part of the world, for there are two pubs, *The Belvedere* on the far side of the hill, and directly opposite you, *Ye Olde Farmhouse*. The dates on it, 1600 – 1892, refer to the farmhouse which stood here and brewed its own beer. Gradually it became an inn, and was eventually rebuilt. To its right you will see a very steep lane, which was the original road out of Bath on this side. Defoe writes of an accident which befell Queen Anne as her coach attempted to climb the hill (which he wrongly calls Kings Down). Apparently the coachman allowed the horses to draw breath, which proved to be an error of judgment, for the whole lot began to roll back, "putting the guards behind it into the utmost confusion, till some of the servants setting their heads and shoulders to the wheels stopt them by plain force". A servant's head seems a rather drastic braking system, and to avoid its further use, the present route was devised as being easier (but not a lot). You should now cross both the roads on your right, although great care will be required because of cars turning from Lansdown Road. Make your way up to the right, past the restored lodge, and before you start ascending the slope into Camden Crescent, look at the house on the end of the terrace, with its beautiful curving balcony. This is *Sheepshank's House*, named after a former owner, and was painted by Sickert. One version can be seen in Burton Agnes Hall in Yorkshire. The garden wall was rebuilt in 1990 after the gales in January of that year when the entire structure came down flat on the pavement. Fortunately nobody was passing at the time.

As you climb, notice the elephants over every doorway from No.7 onwards. Each varies slightly one from the next. This is Camden Crescent, once known as Camden Place, and is named after Charles Pratt, Earl Camden. He was recorder of Bath from 1759 until his death in 1794, and his coat of arms, which includes three elephants' heads, can be seen in the central pediment. At least, it should be central, but if you look carefully, you will see that it is no such thing. As mentioned in 'Street of Strangers', landslips prevented the eastern end from being completed. Like many Bath terraces, building started at each end, so the extreme eastern house had been built, and for many years stood as a romantic ruin at the far end. There are several interesting architectural features. Beneath the triangular pediment there are five columns, to the distress of purists who insist on an even number. The crescent does not stand on level ground, which meant the houses had to be stepped. A glance at the doors and windows will show this to be true,

Camden Crescent from The Paragon, showing the incomplete eastern end. From a print by Nattes, 1806

but it is not immediately obvious because Eveleigh, the architect, disguised it by sloping the features that are normally horizontal, such as the 'platband' or raised flat strip below the first floor windows (2nd floor for American visitors), and the 'entablature' or stonework that sits over the pilasters (or flat columns). The windows have suffered some of the most unsympathetic lengthening of any in Bath during the 19th century. If you can bear to cross the road again, you will get a more complete view of the crescent, and then, by looking over the wall, you will see below you the vaults beneath the street, as described at length in 'Street of Strangers'. The view is fine but a better one is waiting a little higher up the hill. If you crossed the road, return to the northern side, before walking eastwards to the end of the Crescent and turning left up St Stephen's Road at the side.

Avoid steps which date from about 1848 and can be slippery, and as you climb the street you will see a door set in the high wall on the left. If you listen carefully, you may sometimes hear running water. There were many private water companies in the last two centuries, and this was access to the system which served Camden Crescent. Continue to the top of the slope and turn sharp left by the wall. From here there is a fine panorama, which changes as you walk westwards along by the wall towards the top of the steps. You will shortly reach a grassy triangle which marks the top of the old road. From here the road went straight on up the hill, coming out where St Stephen's now stands. Follow the road to the right and on your right you will see the entrance to a house called *Heathfield* which has a rather grand gateway. This is said to be the entrance to John Wood's church which once stood at the south-west corner of Queen Square until it was swept away in 1873 when the Midland Railway Station was built. There are certainly other bits and pieces of columns just behind it in the garden. We shall be taking the road to the left, called Lansdown Grove, but if you look straight up the street you may just make out what appear to be some Tudor chimneys. They are 300 years too young for that, being part of a plan of 1843 by James Wilson. He had intended to build 16 little houses here to be called St. Swithin's Almshouses, but in the event only six were built, and are now called St. Stephen's Villas.

Now take the turning on the left which dates from 1887 when the Bath Land Company developed the ground. Coming into view on your left is a large Victorian building, with decorative terra-cotta tiles at the top, which include the date 1888. The plans by Silcock, a local architect, show the new road and a "Homoeopathic Hospital" on the site. It became the Lansdown Grove House Nursing Institution, linked with the Bath Homeopathic Hospital at No.1 Duke Street. This was "to afford relief to the sick poor of the city" and had a hospital for those from afar. The nursing home was "for those who after recovery from illness still need nursing" and was open to "sick of all classes". The first lady superintendent was Miss Hampshire. It outlived the homeopathic hospital, but is now luxury flats and called *Haygarth Court*. Doctor Haygarth was a well-known medical man in Bath from the 1790s. He is perhaps most famous for setting up one of the first comparative studies using a placebo. Two metal rods stroked over the skin were supposed to be giving patients great relief from pain. Haygarth painted two pieces of wood to look like these metal 'tractors' – and obtained identical results! On your right you will see a garden with what was once a little stone summer-house: it has now been rather swamped by having a large bungalow attached to it. The garden is that of the *Lansdown Grove Hotel*.

Continue down the road until you are opposite the main part of the hotel. Hidden in all the later additions is a Georgian house dated at about 1770, when it appears on a map as Mr. Lloyd's house. The chimney stacks are new, the old ones being further victims of the 1990 gales when they arrived uninvited in the car park. There is a further car park on the left-hand side of the road; from it on a fine day you will obtain a splendid view of the south side of Bath, including *Prior Park*. This was first devastated by fire in 1836, but there was another in 1991; this proved to be an excellent viewing platform. Cross Lansdown Grove towards the hotel, and begin to make your way up the hill. Directly opposite is the main building of Bath High School for Girls. Now known as *Hope House*, its original name was Rock House, the home of Charles Hamilton. He had virtually bankrupted himself in laying out his delightful garden in Surrey called Painshill (now being restored by the Painshill Trust) and he sold up in 1772 and came to

Bath. He lived first at Royal Crescent, but moved here in 1773, acquiring pieces of land between the two homes to lay out another garden. He died in 1786. A sample of his work can be seen locally by visiting Bowood, where he designed the cascade.

Now cross the road and turn left up Lansdown Place East. This is all part of the great double curve which forms Lansdown Crescent, to see the main part of which you now climb until you reach the crest. It is just over 200 years old, being built between 1789 and 1793. The entire development, including the two wings, was known as Lansdown Crescent, the architect probably being John Palmer, and the developers two gentlemen called Spackman and Lowder. There is no doubt that the steeply sloping field in front was intended to be kept open as part of the whole effect, for it was purchased at the same time. The spaces associated with Georgian buildings were as important as the structures themselves. Below the Crescent was a proprietary, or private, chapel called All Saints, in a fanciful Gothick style, to contrast with the Neo-classical above. Experts such as Pevsner tend to dismiss Lansdown Crescent, favouring Royal Crescent, yet most ordinary mortals much prefer the former. Let us stand at this corner where a little lane goes off to the right and look at it in detail. The first thing to notice is that there is a complete set of overthrows or cast iron arches containing street lighting, like the one in the Circus described in 'Windows and Things'. These have been converted to electricity, and now light up automatically every evening, making a most attractive display. Many of the houses also have, hidden among the railings, tradesman's bell-pulls, such as you saw in the Circus. Some houses have sliding wooden shutters. These should not be there, being 19th-century additions, and happily many have been removed. The keystones above the ground-floor windows had to be cut to accommodate them, proving that they are not original. Another addition, although this time a welcome adornment, is the archway at the far end, linking the main part of the crescent with Lansdown Place West. This brings us to probably the most famous resident and great nephew of Charles Hamilton, William Beckford. As we shall see, his influence is to be felt all around this area.

'Alderman' Beckford, William's father, had been one of the wealthiest men in England, his fortune coming from sugar plantations in Jamaica. He bought the Fonthill estate in Wiltshire about 1736, and when he died in 1770, he left one legitimate heir, William, and a number of illegitimate children, the number going up by leaps and bounds from writer to writer: some quote as many as a hundred. Only seven are authenticated. Although William married in 1783 and had two daughters, there was a scandal due to his having been found at night in the bedroom of his cousin, William Courtney. All Beckford's dreams of power and social success were shattered. He then received a further blow when his wife, whom he adored, died in childbirth. He took to travelling, but eventually returned to Fonthill, where he built the fantastic Fonthill Abbey. Fate had not yet finished with him; he

Lansdown Crescent from High Common, showing Cavendish Crescent, Lansdown Crescent, All Saints Church, Cavendish Lodge, Winifred's Dale, and Cavendish Place. From a print by Hollway, 1837

discovered that the agents for his sugar estates had cheated him out of his wealth. He was now thousands of pounds in debt. He therefore sold up Fonthill and came to Bath in 1822. His first intention was to buy *Prior Park*, which fortunately for us he decided was too expensive. Since he had already pulled down one Palladian house, there is little doubt he would have had few qualms about pulling down another. Instead he moved to No.20 Lansdown Crescent and also acquired No.1 of what was then called West Wing. It was he who had the archway added to connect the two, although it seems it did not allow internal access between the houses. The floor of the library contained in the arch is at the same level as the first floor of No.20, but higher than the floor of No.1 West Wing, and butts up against a chimney stack. Beckford rid himself of No.1 about 1831, but acquired No.19 in 1836, ostensibly to keep it empty so that he would not have noisy neighbours. The vacant space proved too tempting, and he moved in. Finally, in the last year of his life, he seems to have rented No.18 as well. In these various homes he kept his collection of books, paintings, and other objects of virtue. Before we leave, and moving from the sublime to the gor blimey, note the grill on the drain at this corner. The individual rungs are numbered proving that the grill was hand made. Each rung was made to measure and numbered accordingly for ease of fitting. Turn right into the narrow lane between the crescent and Lansdown Place East, noticing the wide cobbles, which were laid at crossings to make it more comfortable for pedestrians than the normal narrow ones. Notice too the square metal plate, the coal-hole for No.16. This house has extensive cellars, including one for wine and another for game, but from here coal would be shot straight down into the cellars, to be collected by the maid who would light the fires. Because Bath stone is not very far beneath, part of the cellar wall is a solid limestone boulder.

At the T-junction bear left, and as you do, notice the stones by each corner of the wall. These are touchstones, which would bounce a carriage away from the wall, very necessary here, for the carriage houses were at the back and this was a tight corner to negotiate. There is another at the other end. As you walk up the road, you will see these mews cottages, most now converted into fashionable residences. Some still have cobbled or paved courtyards, and here and there, where conversion has not occurred, you can still see the hayloft doors, with the pulleys for hauling up feed. Not only were these stables, and as such probably home for the grooms and ostlers, but they also seem to have been equipped for making ale. Every house came supplied with a brewhouse. As you walk along, you will eventually come to a larger courtyard on your right, called *Beckford Stables*, with an adjacent house called *Beckford Cottage*. From maps it appears that these were indeed part of his property, although the town houses around the courtyard are modern. Moving further on, you come to another modern development, Dixon Gardens, and here again you meet Beckford. Not content with the garden of No.20, he purchased and leased a strip of land extending for over a mile up the hill in which he laid out grounds of great diversity. At nearly the furthest extent he built *Lansdown Tower*, which can still be visited today. The estate began here with a fruit and vegetable garden on a plot he may have known before he lived here, for it had belonged to his great uncle, Hamilton. If you walk up the cul-de-sac you will begin to see the terraces against which the espaliered trees grew, and up in the right-hand corner you will see what looks like a little castle tower. This is the *Embattled Gateway*, which led on to the rest of the estate. The walk or ride which went up to the gateway was raised up on vaults, in which there is no doubt that animals have been tethered at some time, for the rings are still in the wall. After Beckford's death in 1844, the garden became a sort of Victorian sports centre called the National Gardens. Here people could indulge in archery and bowls and "other Manly Pursuits" including Rackets, the court being roughly where No.2 now stands.

Retrace your steps to the Mews, and continue along. At the corner garden on your left you will see a dome-shaped roof above the wall, topped by the Moorish symbol of the star and crescent. This is the top of the *Islamic Summerhouse* which, because Beckford wrote a Moorish fantasy called *Vathek*, is usually attributed to him. Unfortunately, it does not appear on any map until 1903, and it seems more likely that it was moved here by a later collector who lived in the house, Captain Frederick Huth. The whole corner plot on the other side of the road, from Dixon Gardens onwards and including several modern houses, was all part of the Beckford estate. Turn the corner, and you will see in front of you the archway, topped by urns with genuine fake plants. That is to say, the aloes are made from aluminium and are contemporary with the arch, although recently restored. Go through and turn right down the steep slope. To your left is a little road called All Saints Road, but all that is left of the chapel is a house at the bottom with bits and pieces of decorative masonry included. This area suffered bombing and two craters can still be seen in the field: the chapel fell victim to an incendiary. As you reach a corner, you will see on your right another crescent, Somerset Place. Walk up towards it and stand opposite the centre. Once again we meet Eveleigh, and once again Eveleigh had problems. He began about 1790 with a semi-detached (U.S. duplex) pair of villas beneath the enormous broken pediment decorated with festooned drapery, ribbons, and paterae, or medallions. The central gap is accentuated with an urn. The keystones above the front doors form grotesque faces in what is called icicle-work. Locals believe it was to commemorate a hard winter while building was in progress.

Had Eveleigh stopped here there would have been no problem, but another crescent proved irresistible. Unfortunately there was a slump in building at the end of the 18th century, and the west end was never completed, while the building of the rest lingered on for about 30 years. One attractive feature is that as the houses move further away from the centre, the keystones above the doors become less decorative, until at

The Islamic Summerhouse in the grounds of No.20 Lansdown Crescent

the end they are quite plain. Somerset Place follows on from the line of
Lansdown Crescent so naturally that seen from the air they make a
continuous serpentine shape across the hillside. Continue westwards,
and you will come to a flight of steps on your left. There are three
points of interest to take in as you negotiate these (with care if wet).
The building on your right is called *Somerset House*: until very recently
it bore a sign which said ND BEER. It appears there was once a
connection with the pub and brewery which were further up the lane

on the far side. In the early 1800s it was the home of a builder closely associated with the development of Somerset Place, Thomas Payne. He met his death in 1820 at the age of 75, when he went up to London and was knocked down by a horse and gig. The open space on your left conceals the reservoir for another private water company, Dickenson's, once supplying Cavendish Crescent and Place, which we shall shortly be visiting. The springs became contaminated but they still serve a useful purpose, for they supply the stream in the Botanical Gardens. The access door is in the retaining wall facing the street below. Finally, as you descend you will go under an arch with an electric light. This was originally a gas lamp; the piping can still be seen, and may well date from the time the place was completed. Gas was brought to the city as early as 1818 and to these upper crescents in 1829.

When you reach the bottom you will see a little shop, and above the door you can make out 'Moger's Dairy', named after the tenant in the 1820s, Thomas Moger. There were several Mogers in Bath, including a linen-draper who became a banker. There was even a Moger's Farm further up Lansdown, but that was the banker's elder brother James and not Thomas. The shop was later a greengrocer's, run by a man with the unusual name of Bedggood. Cross the road, and turn left past the end of the shop, noticing the little sign painted on the wall. If you wanted to post a letter here, you are almost 140 years too late! Across to your right you will observe a house in a severe classic style. This is *Doric House*, and together with adjoining houses now lost, was home, gallery and art academy of the artist Thomas Barker. The ground was left to Barker's wife Priscilla by her aunt and in 1803 this small masterpiece of the Greek revival was built to a design by J.M.Gandy. The original design, which was exhibited at the Royal Academy and possibly resulted in Gandy becoming an RA, was rather different, but makes it clear that it was intended purely as a gallery. On the inside of the long wall Barker painted a fresco of *The Massacre at Chios* which still survives. Although Barker bears no comparison with an artist like Gainsborough, his painting of Priscilla, which can be seen in the Holburne of Menstrie Museum at the end of Great Pulteney Street, is an absolute delight.

Continue down the hill, and almost immediately on your left, you will find Cavendish Crescent. This locality was once known as St. Winifred's Dale, for the stream that ran beside it came from the well of that name higher up the hill. Hence this was formerly called Winifred's Crescent. It was built on a plot called Mr. Vivier's garden, which contained two ice-ponds: during a hard winter these would enable people to fill their ice houses ready for a hot summer. Compared with the other crescents you have seen, it is extremely plain, not to say forbidding. In the early years of the 19th century, at the time the area was developed, there was a return to simple elegance across the whole spectrum of fashion: clothes, hairstyles, furniture, and architecture. Pinch, generally considered to be the designer of this terrace, was not always so austere, as we shall see at Cavendish Place, but here we have

Classicism stripped of all but the barest decoration. As at Camden Crescent, there is a rise towards the central house, but Pinch disguises this in the same way as Eveleigh. The window length is right: windows had been getting longer and longer towards the end of the century with improvements in glass (see 'Windows and Things') but they were subsequently shorn of their glazing bars. Happily, these are now being replaced. For almost the first time, the servants up in the garrets have proper windows: the attic storey has been pulled forward to be part of the main composition. From 1830 No.10 was the home of Sir Thomas William Holburne, whose collection of fine art of all kinds forms the basis of the Holburne of Menstrie Museum. He lived here with his three unmarried sisters, gradually filling the house as he attended auctions and sales. Needless to say, he went to the sale of Beckford's property in 1845, and purchased several items. His youngest sister, Mary Anne Barbara, left the collection in trust as a memorial to the family name.

The next plot on the left below the garden of Cavendish Crescent was, at the time of writing, a derelict plot of ground, the *Cavendish Lodge* site. The Lodge was demolished in 1983 after being empty for nearly 20 years, since when it has been the subject of a planning wrangle which has rumbled on ever since. The house dated from 1785, undergoing alteration in 1900, but until early 1994 all proposals for a replacement were rejected due to the sensitivity of the site. This is particularly obvious to anyone who walks up the path across the golf course that can be seen opposite, called High Common, and a popular amenity at weekends. Yet this was nearly lost to the city, as the Council, who owned the land right down to the Upper Bristol Road, was anxious to build, and plans exist from 1827 for an estate reminiscent of Pittville, in Cheltenham, which had been proposed the preceding year. Fortunately it came to nothing, as did the plans two years later for "improvements" which included winding paths and a Carriage Drive, although the footpath down to the park more or less follows its course. Continuing down the hill, we come to Winifred's Dale, a pair of semi-detached villas dating from about 1823 and again thought to be by Pinch. This is the only relic of the old name of this neighbourhood. The building is designed to look like one grand mansion, even to the extent of sharing a porch. Its windows show that it is late Georgian: notice how the frames are curved to fit the bow. The gateposts disagree over the apostrophe 's'. On the next plot, tucked away, is *Cavendish Villa*, part of which is now called *Henrietta House*. A house was built here at the same time as *Cavendish Lodge*, but this is probably a rebuilding. Cavendish Place is next to appear, and this is definitely by Pinch, dating from 1808. It shows Pinch's most striking trade-mark, the bold way in which he deals with the stepping of houses as they climb a slope. Notice how every feature which runs horizontally across the face of each house then sweeps up in a curve to the next. The result is a terrace which seems to ripple up the hillside. The balconies are an original feature, unlike the canopies which some acquired, and which have now been removed. Most have boot-scrapers by the door, to remind us how dirty Georgian streets were. Outside Nos.11 and 6 there are coal-holes in the pavement, each with a groove cut on the upper side of the slope. This was an attempt to stop water running into the cellar, though one wonders how successful it was. Before turning the corner, notice also the post box. The monogram is that of Edward VII. Since he reigned for less than ten years, few of these were made.

Follow the sweep of Cavendish Place left into Park Place, and as you do so, notice that the backs of two houses to your right have plaster over the rubble-stone. That is how the houses should appear, but most have now lost it. Very quickly you arrive in Park Street, and if you look to your left you will see why Dickens, in *Pickwick Papers*, described it as "very much like a perpendicular street a man sees in a dream, which he cannot get up for the life of him". Shunning this impossible task, turn right, which will bring you to St. James's Square. There are some unusual features about it: firstly it is not a square, but an oblong, and the arrangement by which the streets come out at the diagonals is quite odd. There should have been some others like this in Bath, including one where you saw Dixon Gardens, but Bath's bubble had burst, and they were never built. This was designed by John Palmer and erected in the early 1790s on ground used by Royal Crescent residents as an orchard. Needless to say, they were very upset about the loss of space, and one, Christopher Anstey, wrote a poem which ran:

Ye Men of Bath who stately mansions rear
to wait for tenants from the De'il knows where,
Would you pursue a plan that cannot fail,
Erect a Madhouse, and enlarge your Jail.

Today, of course, he would make a planning objection instead, but ironically Bath's architectural fame is due to the fact that the only planning rules were the unofficial ones of taste. About ten years ago this square looked distinctly shabby, but is fast returning to its original splendour. Walk along the top and turn right down the eastern block. You will come to an archway on your left, but before you turn down it, go and look at the southern block. Somehow either Palmer or one of the builders slipped up, and it is not symmetrical about the central design. See if you can work out the error. Return to face the archway.

The square has literary connections, for the writer Walter Savage Landor, who was nearly as famous for his success with women as he was for his writing, contrived to live at no less than four houses, but not at the same time. If you now turn to face the archway, the first of these, No.35, is on your right, and has a plaque to commemorate it. It has another which says that Dickens dwelt there which is at best an exaggeration: he visited Landor, but did not even sleep here! Some believe that Dickens, who was already planning *The Old Curiosity Shop*, used the window you can see through the archway as the model for the shop: clearly the owner thinks so, for it is called *Curiosity Cottage*. There was, however, a shop near Lincoln's Inn Fields in London which would have disputed this. Follow this lane round to the right, and you will find yourself in a delightful courtyard. Turn to face the cottage which looks down it. It is contemporary with the square, and may have been built to house the workmen. It is smaller than it first appears, and was of cheap construction. This is revealed by the use of a bressumer or wooden beam which runs across the top of the ground floor windows. Here it is disguised, as they all should be, by limewash. (For further details on these, see 'Street of Strangers'.) Fixed to the bressumer is a firemark, which unusually retains traces of the original gold and black paint. This proved the house was insured against fire, in this case with the Bath Sun Fire Office. There is a garden running down the eastern side, but the soil is very shallow, for there was a row of little houses here. The coal-holes and gratings show that you are standing over the cellars of the adjoining houses, one of which still has its 'hanging loo', propped up here by metal pillars. These were added during the 19th century as flushing toilets became more efficient and fashionable, but sadly some fell off, with unhappy results for the occupants. It was thus decreed that sturdier methods had to be found of fixing them than timber beams.

Walk out under the attractive 19th-century cast-iron arcade, whose fittings will tell you that there is a butcher's shop here. Turn left on to Julian Road and cross to the grassy triangle. A large church was built here in the early 1870s, the architect being Sir Gilbert Scott. One feature was the spire, the tallest in Bath at 240 feet. Whatever the merits of the building, it was a disastrous position for it, as the steeple destroyed the visual impact of Royal Crescent, immediately to the south. It is for this reason that Pevsner describes it as having been "happily bombed". While excavating for St. Andrew's, substantial Roman remains were discovered, and when the new school was built next to the postwar *St. Andrew's* further relics, including a large, cobbled pavement, were unearthed.

The walk is nearly over, and you might feel like treating yourself to morning coffee or afternoon tea at *The Royal Crescent Hotel*. In that case follow the curve of the coach-houses on the southern side of the triangle and walk down Upper Church Street. The entrance to Royal Crescent is on your right. The hotel is in the middle, but another attraction is No.1, which is run as a museum by the Bath Preservation Trust to demonstrate how a typical Bath town house appeared. If, however, you wish to return to the Assembly Rooms, cross the centre of the triangle and walk down Rivers Street. Turn down to your right just before an inn called *The Chequers*; its stable yard will shortly be seen on your left and retains its original appearance. At the end of the street, turn left and follow the road along and down to the right. You will see the Assembly Rooms directly opposite you, but if you feel like a break from 18th-century architecture, the Museum of East Asian Art is on your right at the bottom of Circus Place. This contains many items of great beauty, which would have been craved by some of the personalities you have met on this walk.

A TRANSPORT OF DELIGHT

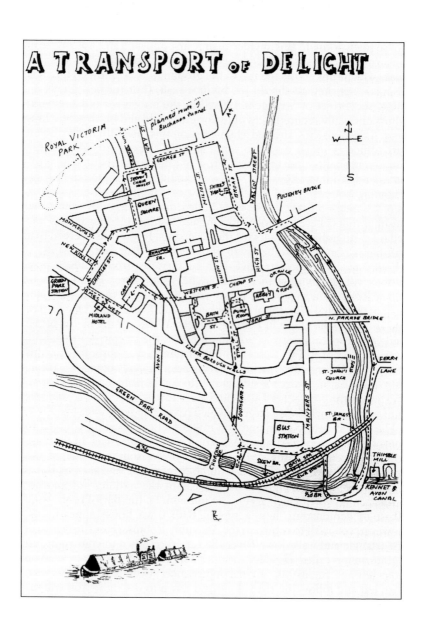

A Transport of Delight

From earliest times, the valley where Bath lies has presented problems for travellers, with its steep hills and meandering river. The Roman army preferred arrow-straight roads subject only to the occasional realignment, but had temporarily to abandon this technique and wander their way into the city. Today the internal combustion engine seems to have made matters worse rather than better. This walk looks at many facets of transport in Bath: actual vehicles; plans and solutions; and some surprising and obscure connections. Ideally, it should be carried out at a time when the *Pump Room* is open to the public.

Start: We begin at the bottom end of Stall Street, on the site of the old South Gate, looking down Southgate Street. Until Pulteney Bridge was built about 1770, this was the only road leading into the city from across the river. It was not, however, the oldest route, for the great Roman road known to us as the Fosse Way crossed the valley. The alignments are clear on the hills on each side of Bath but the course of the road within the city is uncertain. It is possible that it was to the west of the present city centre, coming over Odd Down to Brougham Hayes, crossing the river somewhere in the vicinity of *Green Park Station* (which we shall see later on), the next certain identification being at the northern end of Walcot Street. As with modern roads, there may have been improvements and alterations to allow for changing conditions. The Romans were here, after all, for 350 years. After their departure the city gradually fell into ruin, and the street plan in the modern city centre owes more to the Saxons. This includes the old route from the south, which came down the steep hill called Holloway, described by Leland, writing about 1540, as "a rokky hille fulle of fair springs of water", and across the Old Bridge, of which more later. The 17th-century traveller then came up between open fields and a line of houses, passing on his right the entrance to the Horse Bath, supplied by the outflow from the King's Bath. Though the bath did not last very long, the name lingered on in Southgate Street's alternative name of Horse Street. The bath was used not just for washing the animals, but for curing them as well. The visitor then arrived at the South Gate, which was decorated, so John Wood tells us, with the statue of Edward III, a Bishop as Lord Abbot of Bath, and a Prior. It was demolished in 1755 as Bath burst through its old limits to accommodate its fashionable visitors.

Now turn and walk up the east side of Stall Street passing the wide entrance to Bath Street on your left. Stand by the colonnade which leads into Abbey Church Yard and look across Stall Street. Where you now see a Neo-georgian block of shops, there once stood *The White Hart*. There were, of course, numerous coaching inns in the city: you have already passed the sites of *The Lamb* and *The Three Tuns*, one to each side of Stall Street. The latter had also lodgings in Abbey Green

69

to the east, and this seems to be the basis for the belief that the pub *The Crystal Palace* is in its place. *The White Hart*, however, dwarfed many of the others, with stabling for more than 300 horses, and places for 12 four-horse carriages. It began trade about 1503, and in 1598 the landlord, John Chapman, acquired a house on the other side of Stall Street, roughly where the Mementoes shop is. It became known as "The Hart Lodgings in Staule Street" and appears on Gilmore's map; an elaborate, triple-gabled structure with bays, a grand porch, and a great deal of fanciful stone carving. Wood describes some of the houses in Stall Street as having "the Aspect of as much Magnificence as one would expect to meet with in a King's Palace" and it is possible that this was one he had in mind. When this area was redeveloped in the 1790s the Hart Lodgings disappeared into the *Pump Room* and *Baths*, and the inn was rebuilt. Jane Austen mentions it in *Persuasion* and Dickens lodges Mr. Pickwick and his friends here in *Pickwick Papers*. It is suggested that he derived his hero's name from a landlord, one Moses Pickwick, of which the story is told that he was a foundling, and obtained his name by being *Pick*ed up at *Wick*. Dickens also tells us that the waiters were dressed in tunics, breeches and silk stockings, which, he says, "from their costume, might be mistaken for Westminster (School) boys, only they destroy the illusion by behaving themselves much better". In 1831 it was the scene of a battle. Bristol suffered rioting when it was thought that the Reform Bill was about to be thrown out and troops were brought in to deal with the mob, some being lodged at *The White Hart*. A pro-reform mob attacked the inn to prevent the soldiers reaching Bristol. The defenders put up the shutters, through which the crowd broke, but an unpleasant surprise awaited them, for the troops had armed themselves with red hot pokers, which they applied vigorously. The inn finally disappeared in 1867, when it was replaced by the Grand Pump Room Hotel, a vast manifestation of Victorian exuberance in the French Renaissance style. It was replaced in its turn in 1959 by the present block, called *Arlington House*. Whether or not this was a good thing depends on personal taste. The old inn sign survived, however, and can be seen over the door of the pub of the same name at Widcombe.

These coaching inns were the starting and dropping points for mail and stage coaches, the times being advertised in Bath Guides. Thus we know that in 1813, for example, there were three coaches a day for London from this inn, and six to Bristol, which included the Portsmouth and Oxford mail coaches. If you had just arrived, you took rooms in an inn until such time as you had found lodgings. Once in the city, your chosen form of transport around town was probably the sedan chair, the equivalent of the modern taxi. It was a large box, equipped with a seat, a door at the front, a roof which could be raised, and poles at each side. These enabled it to be carried by two chairmen. It is not known for certain from where the name comes; probably it is of Italian origin, since they are first recorded there. In Bath they were often called glass chairs, referring to the windows on three sides, and Wood refers to Hackney chairmen. There were two ranks or stands in this vicinity: one outside the *Pump Room* and one by the *Abbey*. The colonnade by which you are standing must have been a convenient place to wait in wet weather. We will consider these chairs in more detail in a quieter part of Bath, but if the *Pump Room* is open, you can look at two, and also their replacement. (Even if it is shut, you are advised to read the following paragraph.)

Walk across Abbey Church Yard to the entrance to the *Roman Baths* on the right, cross the hall and enter the Concert Room through the doors directly opposite the entrance. On your left you will see a wheeled vehicle, which is a typical example of the Bath Chair. Wheeled chairs for invalids had made their appearance during the 18th century, and the modern wheelchair still uses the system invented by J.J.Merlin for allowing the occupant to propel himself along. By 1798, chairs like this were being made in Bath, and by 1850 they had completely routed the sedan chair, only to disappear in their turn. In 1937 there were just six left, although the last Bath chairman did not retire until 1949. Leave the Concert Room by the side door to your right, turn left down the passage, then right, which takes you into the *Pump Room*. Immediately on entering, you will see on your right a curved bay, which contains, amongst other things, two sedan chairs without their poles, although the brackets are still visible. One is an example of the public chairs seen in Bath in the 18th century: in plain black leather, it still bears its licence number, 68. The other, elaborately gilded and decorated, is a private chair belonging to a titled owner; notice the coronet. Between them, and under the statue of Beau Nash, is a Tompion clock. This may seem to have no relevance to travel, but in a way it does, for it reminds us that Bath time was not the same as London time. Seconds were added as one moved away from the capital. It was not until the coming of the railways that it was deemed necessary to use GMT throughout the country, although the mail coaches had used London time in addition to local time. Now return to Abbey Church Yard, and make your way back to Bath Street, an elegant example of road widening.

Throughout the 18th century this part of the city had retained its narrow winding lanes. It was decided in the 1790s that these detracted from the city, particularly since a tangle of alleys separated the *Cross* and *Hot Baths* from the *King's Bath*. The old buildings were removed and this graceful street, designed by Thomas Baldwin, replaced them. Pedestrians were given shelter from the notoriously damp western climate by the colonnade. Walk down the street to the *Cross Bath* at the far end. If you were going bathing, you would be collected from your lodgings in a special Sedan chair which seems to have been developed about 1740 by Cleland who worked at the *Mineral Water Hospital*. It looked not unlike a coffin on end, with a bulge at the front to accommodate gouty feet, and the poles were much shorter than normal. The Hospital stills owns possibly the sole survivor. Before that

71

Right: The bathing chair at the Mineral Water Hospital
Bottom left: A full-sized Sedan Chair. Top left: A Bath Chair

time, the chairs used for this service were virtually chairs on poles, with a framework covered in baize and blankets to provide some sort of shelter. This must have proved rather chilly on the return journey, when the bather was wrapped up in blankets and returned, so Celia Fiennes tells us "at your bedside where you go to bed and lay and sweate sometyme as you please".

Now walk to the right of the bath, where you will see an alleyway going northwards, leading to Westgate Street. This is a remnant of the old lanes, for, like many Bath schemes, the redevelopment of this area was never completed. There was going to be a new road here called Nash Street. Go along the alley, turning left at the end until you arrive at a pavement which cuts off access from another road by crossing Westgate Street! This curious arrangement is one of the features of Bath's one-way system, which is principally dedicated to preventing an east/west route through the city centre. It is also the site of the West Gate, the entry point for travellers from Bristol. It was rather grand, and had a large lodging house nestling up against it. Like all the gates, the road through it was narrow, and the pedestrian ways or posterns even more so. They were sometimes called throngs; two could not walk abreast, and the passer-by using them was likely to be jostled and bumped. This happened to the Rev. John Penrose on his visit to Bath in 1767. As he and a group of friends and family were passing through, they were pushed and shouted at by some drunken louts, and Penrose himself was knocked into the wall as one dashed by. A fight developed, in which one of the clergyman's friends wielded his stick to such advantage that the hooligan ended up with a bloody head! Eventually the gate's limitations became intolerable, and it was pulled down in 1776.

Cross the road towards Kingsmead Square and walk westwards along the pavement on the northern side. This will bring you to a flight of steps which leads into Kingsmead Car Park, bringing us to a problem which has not yet found a satisfactory solution, i.e. where to put unoccupied cars. There is no unified plan about parking: the city and county authorities each have a say, not to mention private companies. There are park and ride schemes, which the city would like to extend, but no-one wants a large area of tarmac on their doorstep. Multi-storey car parks are unpopular with planners because of Bath's architectural heritage, although Winchester has succeeded in disguising one as an old mill. The problem is made worse by the fact that most Georgian houses have been turned into flats, without sufficient garaging space. Between the influx of commuters trying to park during the day and flat-dwellers searching for parking space at night, the city is in danger of becoming a massive parking lot. There is one square where the inhabitants, having parked their cars, dare not move them for fear of losing their space. Even the roads through Royal Victoria Park are car-lined rather than tree-lined. Leaving this depressing subject, we shall go and look at a quite different form of transport. Turn left through the car park and go to the left of the modern block at the end. On the other side of the road and to your right you will see a pub called *The Midland*; beyond it is an imposing building in the Palladian style facing down the street. There is a connection, for you are looking at the terminus of the Midland Railway, later part of the LMS. The company had considered coming to Bath in 1846, and 18 years later they decided to build a ten-mile extension from the Bristol–Birmingham main line. Walk up to the corner until you are opposite the station.

Although there were only two platforms, the Midland was clearly out to impress the wealthy visitors it hoped would use the station. They asked local architects to submit plans so that the building would be in sympathy with its Georgian surroundings: perhaps this had an element of being one up on the Great Western, which had opted mainly for a Tudor style. It was, however, a Derby builder and Derbyshire iron-masters who were involved in the construction. Work began on the line in 1868, and by August of the next year, the terminus was being used, although the station was not completed until 1870. Once opened, luxury was the watchword, with chandeliers in the booking hall, and a light, airy train shed, covered by a single span of 60ft. Its correct name was Bath Station, as opposed to Bath Spa, but railway men called it Bath Midland and Bradshaw's Guide sometimes referred to it as Queen Square. Yet this was as far as the company thought it could reach south; the GWR blocked any attempts to extend the line. And then the Somerset and Dorset, known unkindly as the Slow and Dirty, decided to come to Bath, in an effort to boost its fortunes. It had always struggled financially. The Midland Railway welcomed them to the station and by 1874, trains were running from Bath to Bournemouth. Eventually through trains went right up to Manchester and Sheffield, and people still remember with affection the Pines Express, which in the 1920s could whisk you directly to Manchester in four hours, and to Bournemouth in two. The S&D line had problems near the city because of the hills. Two tunnels were necessary: Devonshire Tunnel, a quarter of a mile long, and the Combe Down Tunnel, 1829 yards long. There was also the steep gradient, and this led to the ever-present risk of the footplate men being overcome by fumes in the tunnels or the trains running out of control into the station, yet the only major accident was in 1929. Another danger must have been the S&D engine shed, which was timber. In the age of steam trains it remains a miracle there was not a fire. Sad to say, trains no longer run from the station. The Slow and Dirty was the first to go, when the LMS and Southern jointly took over the running of the line. In 1948 came Nationalisation, and with it the name change to Bath Green Park. For a time, there was a revival in business, but relentlessly it dropped away and in 1966 Dr. Beeching's axe fell, despite vigorous protests. Two events are worthy of mention. In 1961, a feature of Bath Festival had been jazz bands playing in the streets, and a special train ran between Wellow and Bath during the evening of the 9th June with bands at each station, and music on the train. An era ended in 1962 with the final Pines Express, pulled by *Evening Star*. Now the elegant station where a rockery disguised the buffers has found a new role as a meeting place, shopping centre and market, although ironically its western approaches are used as a car park. The old lines are not wasted: the LMS line is used as a cycle track, and part of the S&D has become an open space called the linear park.

Before turning right, cross the road using the lights in front of you. As you walk up Charles Street, look to your left down New King Street, the road on your left with the blocked entrance. On the side of the *Christadelphian Hall* it is just possible to make out an old advertisement for the Marvel Cycle Company. The next turning is unmarked but is called Monmouth Street. After crossing, look down it to the left to the far end where it meets the A4. This was the proposed site of the roundabout leading to the Buchanan tunnel, the scheme put forward in 1964 to carry cross-city traffic from Royal Victoria Park under Gay

Street, Lansdown Road and the Paragon, and coming out on the far side of Walcot Street by the river. Make your way up Chapel Row to Queen Square. As mentioned in some of the other walks, John Wood had built a chapel dedicated to St. Mary at this corner of the square which meant that Chapel Row was virtually a footpath. After the Midland had built the station, it was felt that better access was required, and in 1875 Wood's only church in Bath was demolished. Walk up the western side of the square, cross at the top and continue to Queen's Parade set back on the left, standing outside No.1. This terrace was erected by John Wood the Younger about 1766. It was to the north-west of these houses that the tunnel entrance would have been. Although the scheme was resisted for the best of reasons, not least the loss of Georgian buildings, one wonders now whether some should have been sacrificed to save the rest, especially when one sees the volume of traffic circling Queen Square. Oddly enough there had been a 19th-century plan which would have followed a not dissimilar route, though on the surface. It would have cut in front of Queen's Parade from the Bristol road and joined Gay Street a little higher than the present Queen's Parade Place to your right, through a colonnade. There would have been the loss of some houses in Gay Street, as there were when Queen's Parade Place itself was widened to improve carriage access to the park.

This is now the time to talk a little more about sedan chairs. Walk along Queen's Parade Place towards Gay Street, in front of the steps descending from Gravel Walk. On the right you will see two little houses, each with a chimney. While no-one is completely certain what these are for, the consensus of opinion is that these are chairmen's rests, where they could warm their hands and dry their clothes on a cold, wet day. It would make sense to have them here, for this was a fashionable area to stay, and No.24 Queen Square, behind which these stand, was a very large lodging house with accommodation for about four families. The chairmen had a mixed reputation: although some refer to their kindness, others, including John Wood, speak of their habit of intimi-dating passengers into paying a higher fare, such as the General who was "kept Prisoner in a Chair, with the Top lifted up, in a hard rainy Night till he was as Wet as if he had been immersed in Water". It was for this reason that Nash pressured the council into licensing the chairs and fixing a scale of fares. Fares were double after midnight and in any sixpenny fare, the passenger was entitled to ask for up to ten minutes stop without extra charge. Since it was in the chairmen's interests to complete a journey as quickly as possible, stopping to chat was extremely unpopular with them which is why there had to be legislation. The desire for celerity also meant that they tended to go everywhere at the trot, and the wise pedestrian kept clear of corners for fear of meeting a chair coming at top speed in the other direction. At night a little boy called a link-boy ran in front of the chair with a flaming torch or link to light the way. Some houses in Bath still have iron cones, called link-snuffers, by their doors where torches were extinguished. Though the chairmen acted as a police force at night, they too fell foul of the law by indulging in fighting and assault. The most common misdemeanour was swearing. Sometimes they were the victims, vandalism to the chairs being not uncommon. There were also complaints that the chairs became sodden in the rain; certainly the chairmen must have done, despite their uniform of blue waterproof greatcoat and large cocked hat. A place to dry out must have been very welcome.

Continue to Gay Street, which should be crossed with great caution before turning left and then right along George Street. This will bring you to the top of Milsom Street, which is now one-way, the traffic going down the hill, but in 1897 it was one-way in the opposite direction. It has an odd arrangement at the entrance to the street which is supposed to 'calm' the traffic. Continue along George Street, past the *Royal York Hotel*, turning right into Broad Street. There are two stable yards off this street, one now used as Broad Street Car Park, which we shall look at in some detail in the final walk, and one used as the entrance to a shopping precinct called Shire's Yard. More importantly there is the Postal Museum at No.8. As mentioned in 'Street of Strangers', Bath has many connections with the development of the postal service. The invention of the mail coach was one, and it came about because of the activities of the theatre owner/manager John Palmer (not to be confused with the architect of the same name). His experiences in travelling round the country recruiting and relocating actors convinced him that there was scope for improvement in the postal service, both in speed and security. It is hard for us to realise how difficult and dangerous travel was. The roads were frequently in an appalling state, which is why turnpike or toll roads came into existence. The toll paid for the upkeep of the road, but could not offer protection from highwaymen, who were not a romantic legend, but a very real threat. Palmer finally persuaded the Postal Service to adopt a system of coaches that was speedy, punctual, and carried armed guards. Their punctuality was their defence, for if they did not arrive at the next staging post by an appointed time, a hue and cry would be raised. The first coach ran on 2nd August 1784, leaving Bristol at 4pm, Bath at 5.20, and arriving at Lombard Street in London about 9am. The museum traces the story of postal deliveries and has some fine route maps.

Continue down Broad Street, noting *The Saracen's Head* on your left, another coaching inn. Beyond it is *St. Michael's Church*. There was a stand here for hackney carriages which were introduced in 1829, an event which caused great dismay among the sedan chairmen. They were considerably cheaper than chairs, and, if hiring by time, the hirer was entitled to demand a minimum speed of 4mph. The stands were strategically placed, some out as far as Lansdown Crescent and Grosvenor: this was the most central. Using the crossing lights, make your way to *The Podium*. As you face the *Abbey* you are looking down Northgate Street where stood what Leland called the Town Gate.

According to Wood, it had a statue of Bladud, the legendary founder of the city, which was so neglected by the City Council that after complaints it was replaced by another. This, Wood says, was "PAINTED TO THE LIFE; it looks however more like a dressed Puppet, seated in a Ducking Stool, than the figure of a famous King". Wood could never resist a swipe at the Council so you can judge the accuracy of his criticism by visiting the *King's Bath*, where the statue of Bladud is thought to be the one from the gate. Like the South Gate, the Town Gate was removed in 1755 in yet another road-widening scheme. Follow the road around the corner into Bridge Street and walk down over *Pulteney Bridge*.

Until the Pulteney family decided to develop their estates on the east side of the city, the only bridge over the river had been the one to the south, although the New Bridge had been built well to the west of the city in 1735. The Pulteneys first employed the architect Robert Adam, the great man of the latter half of the 18th century. Although they subsequently rejected his plans for the estate, they accepted the design for the bridge. Despite being frequently compared with the Ponte Vecchio in Florence, Adam really based it on a design Palladio made for the Rialto Bridge in Venice. In many ways, *Pulteney Bridge* was not a success. It was too narrow, creating difficulties when the street beyond it was built, and not only did it bankrupt the builder, Reed, but it began to show ominous signs of subsidence just four years after its completion. It continued to give problems for the next 25 years or so, to such an extent that consideration was given to pulling it down and building a new one. Eventually Pinch rebuilt the northern side in 1801; if you look carefully you will see it really is quite different from the southern range. Since then occasional repairs have been necessary, such as strengthening the foundations, which was carried out in 1969, and at the time of writing traffic restrictions have been placed on it. The next bridge was not built until 1827, and is the *Cleveland Bridge*, linking Bathwick with the London Road. Before moving on, you should glance down Great Pulteney Street where, at the far end, you will see the Holburne of Menstrie Museum and behind it the trees in Sydney Gardens. It was from here in 1802 that the first balloon ascent in the city was made by a Monsieur Garnerin. The first centenary was celebrated with a reconstruction of the event organised by Patrick Alexander, a local aviation enthusiast. The next day he took a group to Lansdown to watch an experimental unpowered flying machine. Among the on-lookers were the brother of Baden-Powell, Charles Rolls of Rolls Royce, and Sam Cody, an American often muddled with Buffalo Bill Cody. (He did much to foster this confusion.) Cody brought his innovative ideas on flying to this country, and was a founder of the Royal Flying Corps. Hot air balloons are still to be seen above the city but today we are accustomed to seeing them taking off from Royal Victoria Park. Cross the road and by the last shop on the bridge you will see a flight of steps marked 'Riverside Walk'. Descend here, and you will come out by the river. Walk beside the river to the modern sluice gate and climb up on to the platform .

For a city restricted on two sides by a river it seems natural to use the waterway itself for transport. Unfortunately this became impossible from as early as the Saxon period when mills were built beside the river. With the mills came weirs, which are really dams to channel water into the millrace when water levels are low. They caused the river to be inaccessible to boats, particularly from Bristol. There were two mills here, one on each side of the river, with the weir running diagonally across between them. If you look directly across the river to Parade Gardens you will see, just south of the colonnade, a small structure overgrown with creepers, all that is left of Monks' Mill. Throughout the ensuing centuries the mill-owners resisted attempts to make the river navigable, despite pathetic pleas from the city complaining of the "rockie and mountaynous waies" between Bath and Bristol. There was, however, a ferry here, slightly upstream of *Pulteney Bridge*. On Savile's map the boatman can be seen pulling the ferry across by a rope which ran across the river. When Spring Gardens were opened by Mr. Purdie, where you can see the stands of Bath Rugby Football Club, a new ferry came into operation below the weir. It started on the far side from a roadway made to unload the stone for building Queen Square, seems to have landed just below where you are standing, and is described as "A Commodious Pleasure Boat". Although Pulteney's bridge finally rendered this ferry unnecessary by allowing chair and carriage access to the gardens from the city, the boat was used in a dramatic rescue in 1772. The newspaper account runs: "A Boat with two women was carried down the river, then in flood, through an arch of the new bridge, passing over the weir safely, the boat was carried back by the reflux of the water under the weir and swamped. – one woman was rescued by a boat from the Mill, the other by Mr. Purdie, who put off in his boat to her assistance." Even today this modern weir, which allows increased water flow in times of flood, can and does claim victims. Now leave your viewpoint and return to the river bank. Where the moorings begin you will see some steps to the river. Here there is a plaque which records the fact that the river finally opened to navigation in December 1727.

There had been many schemes to open up the Avon, including one in 1626 by Henry Briggs of Oxford University, who had noticed that at one point the Avon and the Thames are only three miles apart. After his unexpectedly early death, his friend Francis Mathew campaigned for the scheme, which he foresaw could bring coal from the Forest of Dean down the Severn, up the Avon to the Thames, and finally into London. This gives an idea of the problems of taking freight by road at that time. Unfortunately the outbreak of the Civil War in 1643 caused the plan to collapse. Later attempts to open up the river met with opposition not just from the mill-owners who feared for their water supply but by shop-keepers resisting cheap competition. It was even suggested that crowds would be attracted by this new trade and "a great concourse of People may very well prejudice the Health of the Bath and the Accommodations of those who have occasion to make use of their Waters". The Corporation pointed out that it would be "very Beneficial to Trade ... advantagious to the Poor, and convenient for the carriage of Free-Stone, Wood Timber, and other Goods and Merchandise" but to no avail. Finally Ralph Allen and the Duke of Beaufort joined forces with others including a Bristol timber merchant called Hobbs, and their influence and business enterprise proved irresistible. The Avon Navigation became fact. It was not without its ups and downs. It had no horse-towing path until 1812; the boats were hauled by teams of men. In 1738 Saltford Lock was blown up by Somerset miners hoping to prevent the import of Shropshire coal. Despite a reward the perpetrators were never caught, which was just as well, because interfering with the works of a navigable river carried the death penalty.

The next bridge we come to is *North Parade Bridge*, built in 1836. This was an iron bridge, but the girders have been hidden with a stone facing and concrete slabs under the arch. The toll-houses can be seen away to your left; little Jacobethan fancies by Edward Davis. Passing under it and looking across the river, you notice John Wood's terraces, North and South Parade. From the end of the street in front of the latter you can see a flight of steps descending to the river. These replace the old Whitehall steps, which led to the ferry of the same name; the road you will soon see on your left is still called Ferry Lane. It was used by people going to Widcombe and Lyncombe, as Penrose did, or by those such as Fanny Burney who decided to take a walk through the meadows to Bathwick. The next building on the far bank is *St John's Roman Catholic Church*; it too has a transport connection, being designed by C.F.Hansom of Bristol, younger brother of the inventor of the Hansom cab.

The next bridge introduces us at last to the Great Western Railway, and that brilliant engineer, Isambard Kingdom Brunel. He avoided coming through the centre of the city by keeping to the south, but since the station itself was on the north bank, he had to cross the river twice to reach it, once on each side. This is the easterly crossing, a bold single span still pretty much as Brunel designed it, supported by side arches now used as workshops. We shall meet the railway again, but first follow the path by the river, eventually reaching the canal and crossing it on a small bridge. If you look over the bridge you will see the first lock, yet puzzlingly this is not Lock No.1. The Kennet and Avon Canal is made up of three waterways: the Kennet Navigation from Reading to Newbury, built initially by 1723, though repairs were necessary in 1734; the Avon Navigation, from Bath to Hanham, the first village upstream of Bristol to have had a mill; and the canal proper. This ran from Newbury to Bath on which work began in 1794, although it was not until 1810 that it was complete. Like a motorway, as sections were built they came into use, and at Devizes a horse-drawn tramway allowed traffic until the completion of the last section, the massive flight of 29 locks, of which 17 follow one immediately after another. The canal company acquired control of the Avon Navigation in 1796, so the river from Bath to Hanham, with its six locks, is part of the canal. In 1813, the guide book said: "This canal supersedes in a great measure the other modes of carriage, and will at least relieve humanity from the pain of witnessing those repeated instances of cruelty which the barbarity of the collier inflicts on his wretched animals." It seems an odd advertisement for a canal, but it should be remembered that canal horses were subject to regulations, so they had a better life than a carrier's animal. Boats carrying 60 tons could make a smooth journey between Bath and Newbury in about three days, and once a French packet carrying linen drapery came from London down the canal to Bristol. For many years the K&A was a profitable enterprise, boosted by trade from the Somersetshire Coal Canal, but a competitor was on its way: the railway. After a long decline, the canal has been restored, and now provides a pleasurable cross-country route for boaters and walkers. The building by the lock is *Thimble Mill*, an old mill taken over by the canal company in the 1830s to pump water back up the Widcombe flight; it proved unsuccessful and was abandoned a few years later.

Walking away from the canal and riverside up to the road and turning right, we come to a foot-bridge over the river. This is a replacement after the original, made of timber and based on Brunel's Saltash Bridge, collapsed into the river in 1877. The Weymouth train came in full of visitors for the Bath and West Show on Beechen Cliff; they crammed on to the toll bridge, the toll being collected at the far end from the station. "The flooring of the bridge was seen to bend, a crash followed, ... and the holiday crowd previously standing on the bridge were suddenly shot ... into the centre of the river Avon. Others fell on the tow-path, and others were buried beneath the falling debris." There were ten deaths and 40 to 50 injured. The bridge is still known as the *Halfpenny Bridge*, the amount of the toll. Perhaps Bath is obsessed with calamity, for marked in the wall beneath the bridge are various extreme flood levels. Part of this area was a poor part of town known as Dolemeads, where Ralph Allen, postmaster, mayor, and quarry owner, had his wharf. The stone was brought down a tramway from Combe Down and loaded by Mr. Padmore's Patent Crane into boats. (This is discussed at greater depth in 'A Most Charming Prospect'.) Cross the bridge and follow the signs to the city centre under the arches to your right, taking you beneath the railway line. Stand on the far side of the road, by the hotel and look back at the station.

The GWR, or God's Wonderful Railway, came to Bath in 1840, the line to London being fully opened in 1841. The excitement this engendered can really only be experienced by reading contemporary accounts: the guide book of 1843 speaks of "this stupendous undertaking" and narrates the problems faced by Box Hill, when "MR. BRUNEL, with that Napoleon-like boldness for which he is so celebrated" built a tunnel 1.75 miles in length. It does not tell you that some people were so frightened of it that an enterprising coach owner took people from Corsham to the next western station to avoid it, nor that nearly 100 men lost their lives in constructing the line. It was, of course, broad gauge: according to Brunel this gave scope for higher speeds and greater stability. His test of a well-built line was one where he could sit in his special carriage in a train going at full speed and write in his normal hand-writing. Eventually standard gauge won the day, principally for reasons of economy, but passengers travelling on an Intercity 125 at full speed may regret that victory. Throughout the line Brunel had preferred architecture in the Tudor style, and so the station has the appearance of an Elizabethan manor. Internally it once had a glass roof which covered all four lines, but it was removed in 1890 and the platforms widened, covering the site of the two outer lines. Today the standard-gauge tracks sit forlornly in the broad-gauge gap. A footbridge ran from the station across to the hotel for the convenience of guests. The access from the platform can still be seen above the arch you used. One writer has suggested it should be called the Garibaldi Bridge, for when he came through by train, in 1864, it was intended that he address the crowds from here. The crush on the platform was so great, however, that he was unable to dismount from the train! Turning to an entirely different form of transport, the street that runs up into the city from the station is Manvers Street and it was in premises here, in 1912, that a biplane was constructed in three weeks by a Mr. Bush. It was flown locally, and was called 'The Bath and London Motor Plane'. Now cross back to the station, and walk westwards along Dorchester Street. On your right you will see the bus station, the only part of the Abercrombie plan to be built apart from the abattoir. (For more details on this scheme, see 'Street of Strangers'.)

Continue to the end of Dorchester Street, follow the pavement round to the left, and you will see a wide footbridge on your left, on which you should stand. From here you can see the great pseudo-Tudor viaduct by which the GWR crossed town. At least, it is Tudor on this side, which faced the wealthy parts of the city. The other side, over-looked by poorer parts, is plain and brick-built. However, the poor were not neglected. On the Lower Bristol Road the viaduct has little houses built into it, but even the most destitute felt they could not live under a railway. Here there is a rather attractive circular decoration which resembles closely a wheel. Beneath it was a police and fire station, which later became a greengrocer's shop. Another small arch to the west was a mortuary, used for bodies pulled out of the river. It was up to the duty policeman to lay the body out for post-mortem. Modern susceptibilities resulted in the word 'Mortuary' being removed in 1961. All the arches were once pointed Gothic but about 1911, when heavier engines were introduced, the railway company strengthened the viaduct by replacing them with girders, as you see today. It is sometimes said that they were removed due to the requirements of trams or buses.

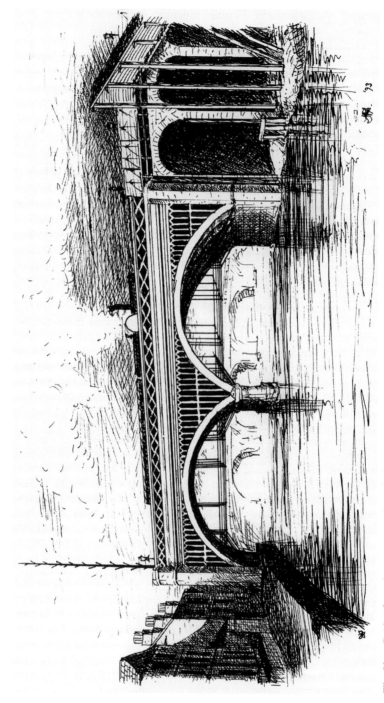

The Skew Bridge from the upstream side with the Old (or St Lawrence's) Bridge visible through the spans

Electric trams had run under the arches on single tracks since their introduction in 1904; the earlier horse trams, dating from 1880, had been a very localised affair avoiding hills. Eventually, about 1935, trams were replaced by double-decker buses. An increase in road traffic may have been behind a plan which seems to have been mooted about 1929–30. There are, in the Bath City Archives, two old photographs of about that date which have had a pencil sketch made on them to show what the area would look like if the whole central portion of the viaduct were removed. In its place was to have gone a metal bridge of two spans, looking like two Sydney Harbour Bridges end to end. To your left is the bridge by which the railway crosses over the river. Called the *Skew Bridge*, it is the second on the site. The 1843 guide book called the first one "a masterpiece of ingenuity and science" but a guide book of 1864 is dismissive: "The Railway Bridges at Bath display great, but unnecessary, ingenuity, and show how a simple, and inexpensive object has been effected by means both complicated and costly. The Skew Bridge … is borrowed from the American railways, in which the material is generally wood." In fact it was made of laminated timber, a two span arch of great beauty. The wood was preserved by a method called Kyanising, and it worked well, for it outlived its projected life span by 15 years. It was replaced in 1878 after the *Halfpenny Bridge* tragedy amongst worries about wooden bridges, but this girder bridge in wrought-iron uses the original pier in midstream.

Finally we come full circle by considering the Old Bridge mentioned at the start. Called St Lawrence's Bridge, it dated from 1362, and had five arches, a chapel, and defensive gates. Since some of Bath's water supply came from the south side of town, there was a water-pipe which crossed the bridge; it had a hole or 'suspra' at the highest point to prevent air-locks. The bridge stood almost unaltered until it was rebuilt in 1754, although some of the old carvings were retained; it is thought they were thrown into the river in 1799. Mindless hooliganism is not new! It was then widened in the 1880s and a pierced iron parapet added at each side. And there it stood, still with its five arches, although these added to the repeated flooding in this part of town by restricting the flow of water. Finally, in 1960 there was one flood too many and it was declared unsafe. The army built a Bailey bridge just downstream and the Old Bridge was strengthened by a sort of lump in the middle; traffic operated on a one-way system between them while the *Churchill Road* and *Foot Bridges* were constructed on each side of the old one. As you look down Southgate Street you will notice that it meets neither of the new bridges; it is still trying to meet the old one as it had done for 600 years. Since the modern Southgate is a pedestrian precinct, we return to the city centre on the oldest form of transport of all: foot.

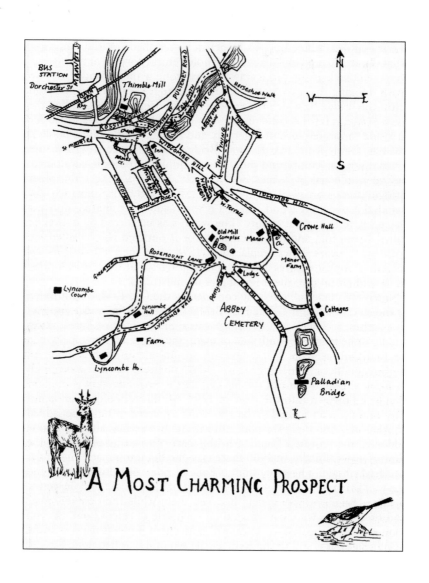

A MOST CHARMING PROSPECT

A Most Charming Prospect

In this walk we explore Lyncombe and Widcombe, a part of Bath that is historic as well as pretty, with a great variety of scenery. The title comes from Fielding's book *Tom Jones*, and is part of the description of Squire Allworthy's estate, which, it is suggested, was based loosely on *Prior Park*, home of Ralph Allen, the man who dominates this part of Bath. At the age of 19 the Cornishman was appointed Postmaster of Bath. He modernised the postal service, running it with a combination of business competence and moral rectitude. Not only did he make his own fortune, but he made a gift to the country of a reliable service, without the corruption and inefficiency which had dogged its previous history. He then expanded his interests, most notably by buying up the stone quarries to the south of the city and developing the Bath stone industry. The wealth from these interests allowed him to purchase the hillsides above Widcombe, and lay out the great estate of *Prior Park*. As we shall see, Fielding knew Allen well. This walk is full of views, some open and some just glimpsed. It is also a walk where you are never far from water; John Wood says that Lyncombe means watery valley, and another authority says Widcombe means valley of the withies (or willows). Although it is an attractive walk at any time, the valleys are seen at their best in spring and autumn.

Start: We begin where the canal meets the river at a lock beside *Thimble Mill*. It is not certain where the name came from; one theory is that the mill either produced 'thimbles', or bobbins, used in the weaving trade, or spun thread on to them. From here they could be shipped up to Bradford on Avon. As mentioned in 'A Transport of Delight', it was unsuccessfully used by the canal company to pump water back up the waterway, after 20 years of struggling with poor water supplies at the Widcombe flight. The scheme only worked when the company opened the bottom lock gates and pumped from the river. The mill-owners further downstream soon noticed the drop in water-supply and forced the company to stop. The canal basin provided an extra reservoir of water; there are others on the way up the flight. One can only regret that the basin does not have a more attractive setting, but it was always a poor area called Dolemeads. Despite fanciful street names, the homes were so liable to flooding that the area became known as Mud Island. Eventually it was rebuilt about the turn of this century, with a variety of well-designed cottages. If you want to get some idea of the floods, you should walk along the river bank until you are standing under the footbridge called *Halfpenny Bridge*, (whose story is also told in 'A Transport of Delight'.) There you will see some past flood levels marked on the wall. However the route of this walk takes the canal tow-path.

Go under the road bridge (tall people beware!) and notice to your right the *Ebenezer Baptist Chapel* dating from 1820, with charming Gothick windows. It acquired a certain notoriety for the texts painted on the roof, which you may glimpse from time to time. It stands in a terrace which was originally much longer, and fronted the canal. (In the 1978 report *Saving Bath* the planning department commented that there was an uneasy transition of scale between the bulk of the Baptist Chapel and the remaining small-scale houses. Considering some of the post-war developments approved by the Council, this is quite amusing.) Continue along the tow-path, under the arch of another low road bridge, through which you cannot fail to notice two enormous lock gates looking like a gloomy cliff across the canal. This is Widcombe Deep Lock, one of the deepest in the country; it takes half an hour to fill and replaces locks 8 and 9, lost, along with many other features, when Rossiter Road was carved through Widcombe in the 1960s. Climb up the steps to your right and cross to the other side of the lock; you can use the footway on the gates if you feel secure about doing so. Above the lock is a reservoir, and by continuing along the tow-path you reach another lock. This has a pretty iron bridge, which at the time of writing is in some need of restoration. There are two of these; the other is further up the flight. It is thought they were added to the lock as a safety measure: people crossing on the lock gates were slipping and falling in. It can be seen that it rests on the walls at the tail of the lock, rather than being an integral part. Both were made locally by a firm called Stotherts, later to become Stothert and Pitts. Resume your walk along the tow-path, and you will soon see a bridge crossing the canal. Climb up to the road, noticing the metal bars on top of the bridge, which allowed the towing ropes on the old narrowboats to slide easily across. Turn right, but stop as you reach the end of the bridge, opposite the sign that tells you this is Horseshoe Walk. Look to your left, where, on the far side of the canal, is what appears to be an obelisk topped with an urn.

This oddity was once a chimney, and is all that remains of the upper of two pumping stations, of which *Thimble Mill* was the lower. Now the canal is open again, the site is something of a general service station for passing boats. Just in front of you is one of the old diamond-shaped warning signs erected in compliance with the Road Traffic Acts of 1896 and 1902 by the Great Western Railway, who owned the canal by then. To prove it, they used a spare piece of railway line as the support. As you turn away from the canal and round the corner by *Abbey View House*, you will see that you are in for a climb, but to give you a break, turn right into the cul de sac called Abbey View Gardens. From time to time you will have caught glimpses of the city, but here, above the allotments, there is a fine view across to the slopes of Lansdown. In the foreground are the brick-built cottages on the old Dolemeads site. Return to the hill and make your way up to The Tyning. Before you turn into it, notice the open space on your left. There is a sign here that states that ball games are prohibited; from the steepness of the slope one would guess that ball games are probably *impossible*.

Walk the length of The Tyning, which has solid late Victorian houses on the right. Though influenced by many architectural styles, they have considerable charm. The last house has a pretty porch with a foxy windvane. At the far end, cross the road, turn right and left into Widcombe Crescent, built about 1805 by Harcourt Masters. This is probably one of the most unusual crescents in Bath, being inside out, i.e. the fronts face away from the view. There are other unconventional features to observe as you walk round, but before passing No.1, notice the plaque to Sir James Brooke, "The First Rajah of Sarawak", who lived here from 1831 to 1834. The ground-floor window has a most attractive arrangement of glazing bars. Now walk slowly along, looking at the façade. The front doors are arranged in pairs under a unifying arch, above which are triple-light windows. They look rather odd; the central one is blind, because the stair-case and party wall is behind it, and a portion of the banisters can be seen on each side. Some architectural experts enthuse about this crescent, and one is forced to ask why. On this side it is rather small and dark, but on the other it is a veritable cliff. Would it get planning permission today? The reversal of the rooms, so that the principal rooms are at the back, results in the glimpse of the staircase in those fussy central windows, and the decoration in the entrance arches, described as a floral boss, resembles more closely a cabbage. To be fair, this could be caused by accretions of paint, for the one on the last pair of houses has been restored and is far daintier.

Facing the end house is Widcombe Terrace, built at the same time and attributed to the same architect. Can this be right? The styles are so different that it seems hardly credible. The first feature that you notice is the double bay at the end, the curved window frames characteristic for a building of this date. The fronts, which gaze boldly across a vaulted pavement at a stunning view, have an architectural confidence lacking at the crescent. These houses are actually smaller then their neighbours, but they appear grander. One has had a balcony added, but the delicacy of its ironwork prevents it from looking out of place. Surely, with its Vitruvian scroll, the arched entrances set in rustication, the recessed window arches on the first floor, this building says Baldwin? Although we know that Harcourt Masters was actively involved in this development, we also know he had capitalised on a Baldwin design at Sydney Gardens. Has the same thing happened here? Take the time to admire the view from the pavement which looks right across the valleys before walking past the end with the double bay to find a steep flight of steps. Climb these to take you up to Church Street.

Once there was a pub and brewery called *The New Inn* at the junction; it appears on Thorpe's map of 1742, but was demolished in 1923. The wall of No.1 Widcombe Hill still bears the marks where the inn was attached, including part of a cornice. As you walk along Church Street, you first pass on your right the back doors of Widcombe Terrace, before reaching *Somerset House*. Towards the beginning of this century it was the vicarage, but before that it was 1, 2, and 3 Widcombe Villas. Some parts of the interior date from the 1720s. Mowbray Green suggested, rather controversially, that although looking quite grand now, they were originally cottages built by Ralph Allen for his workmen. We shall see some examples of such cottages later. Further along on your left you will see Nos.11 and 12, which date from at least the 1600s and possibly earlier. They still retain the old casement windows with mullions. On your right you will pass a house called *Widcombe Lodge*. This stands on the site of the original vicarage called Yew Cottage, from a venerable tree that stood in the grounds. In the late 19th century the tree was chopped down and the house enlarged to the point of complete change, to the disgust of Tyte, writing in 1917. He described it as the replacement of the picturesque by the commonplace. There is a plaque which states that Sarah and Henry Fielding stayed here. To be more accurate, the old house was Sarah's home, Henry living at Twerton in a house (now demolished) where he is believed to have written much of *Tom Jones*. Ralph Allen acted as their patron, and Fielding often stayed with his sister when mixing with society at *Prior Park*. Sarah was a novelist in her own right, pioneering the idea of children's literature. Another novelist is associated with the plaque, for it was unveiled by Sir Arthur Conan Doyle.

By now you will have *Widcombe Parish Church* in your sights. This is one of the most delightful corners of Bath, and its peaceful air may be due to the fact that this has been a place of worship for over a thousand years. The Saxons had a chapel here, from which the only survival is the Gospel Book, now kept in Corpus Christi College, Cambridge. It was replaced by a Norman church dedicated to Thomas à Becket. About 1490 that too was replaced by the present church, built by John Cantlow, Prior of Bath Abbey. (There are still members of this family living in Bath today, though it is now spelled Cantello, one of whom describes the prior as the white sheep of the family!) In the late 16th century the City Council was busy acquiring by fair means or foul the property of the churches in their grasp. They therefore tried to close Widcombe church, but the congregation took legal action to prevent this. In the 18th century repairs and additions took place, including galleries paid for by Ralph Allen so that his workmen at Combe Down and Dolemeads could attend. There was a further attempt to close the church in 1861, when the cost of repairs appeared prohibitive, but once again the parishioners protested successfully. A restoration fund was set up which allowed not only repairs but improvements. Sadly but understandably, it is now kept locked, so that its interior features cannot be seen. This is a pity, for the windows alone merit a visit. They contain pictures of shrubs, plants and flowers referred to in the Bible.

Walk up to the porch and turn sharp left up the steep stone steps set in the grass. This will allow you to walk around the east end of the church to take in the view to the west. As you turn westwards you will notice a strangely shaped building intruding into the churchyard. This is the *Garden House* in the grounds of the *Manor Farm*, a building whose façade is of such grace and elegance that some think it may be by John

Wood. When you reach the edge of the churchyard, you have below you *Widcombe Manor House*, sometimes called the Golden House. What was once its estate is all around you. In the distance you can see an ornamental cascade, which also served a useful purpose, as we shall see later. To your left is *Manor Farm*, its grounds now a beautiful garden. The farm also has a dovecote, which you may glimpse later on. Just to the left of where you are standing is the grave of Horace Annesley Vachell who lived at *Widcombe Manor* until his death in 1955. He loved the estate, and he lies here, overlooking its beauties.

In order to look closer at *Widcombe Manor*, retrace your steps to the church gate and turn sharp left along the road. At one point you will have to step into the road to avoid a buttress of the tower; this prevented the road widening which was proposed here in the early years of this century. You will find the gates of the Manor House on your right. In the 17th century there had been a mansion here, built by Walter Chapman, a name that recurs in the Council minutes. The Chapmans were one of the most powerful families in Bath; part of the north aisle of *Bath Abbey* is known as the Chapman Aisle because so many lie buried there. They were great benefactors to the Abbey. Gilmore's map shows that members of the family owned substantial lodging houses in the city. One, William, was Chamberlain and then Mayor in the mid-18th century, and Thomas Baldwin, City Architect, married Elizabeth Chapman. All in all, it was useful to be connected to them, and in 1702, Jane, daughter of the splendidly named Scarborough Chapman, married one Philip Bennet. It was his son, also Philip, who built the basis for the present house, about which there is considerable speculation. The usual date given for his rebuilding of the old house is 1727, but there is evidence to indicate that it was later than this. Even the architect is unknown. Several authorities suggest Greenway, who had built Nash's House in the Sawclose. Others say it is too splendid to be his work. Whoever it was, this is certainly a masterpiece. Its rich decoration includes the 'green men' in the keystones of the windows, and garlands and cornucopiae around the oval window in the pediment. It still has the stone tiles characteristic of its early date. In the 19th century it was extended, the architect James Wilson skilfully and unobtrusively blending his work on to the old house. The fountain which stands in the courtyard is thought to be Italian work of the renaissance period, imported to its present site by an early 20th-century owner. From this vantage point, you can just see the front of the garden house in the grounds of *Manor Farm*.

Return to the church, where you are about to turn sharp right around to take you up Church Lane. As you make the turn, you get a good view of the church tower, which is embellished with a number of coats of arms. Those of *Bath Abbey* are above the porch; the stone may come from the earlier Norman church. Hidden in the trees on the far side of the porch are Prior Cantlow's arms, and on the east side are the arms of the Priory of Bath, a mitre and a weaver's shuttle. It was the French monks who had introduced weaving to the city. The grounds on the left of Church Lane are those of *Crowe Hall*, built about 1760 or 1770 for a Mrs. Barbara Crow. It had an enormous portico added in the 1870s, and the Tugwell family, who owned it from 1804 to 1919, also sought the advice of William Carmichael, the gardener at Sandringham, when landscaping the gardens. From time to time it is open under the National Gardens Scheme, the entrance being in Widcombe Hill. The locked gate in the wall leads into an extension to Widcombe's graveyard, bought in 1782, and now disused, except by a local beekeeper. The lane is said to be an old pack route to Salisbury: it later turns into a footpath, and the line of it certainly picks up other pack routes into Somerset and Wiltshire. Once it was the only way out of this valley, but about 1730 Philip Bennet reached an agreement with Ralph Allen to continue Church Street as a carriage road, linking up with Allen's new carriage road from *Prior Park*. Opposite the Manor Farm buildings is *Gothic Cottage* – Victorian Gothic! It has a date of 1854. You now have a pleasant walk through rural surroundings. You can hear the sound of water as it falls over a small cascade in the field below, and you may well see birds such as grey wagtails. If you are very quiet you may catch sight of some wild deer. Eventually you come to a house called *Strawberry Gardens*, where once strawberries were grown. By now the lane is about to turn into a track, and to your right are some modern houses. To your left is *Allen's Cottage*, with the inscription PW 1799. It is said not to have any connection with Ralph Allen. In front of you is a gate, through which you can see the grounds of *Prior Park*. These were given to the National Trust in 1993 and are being restored; there is, however, no public access from this gate. It is hoped that the grounds will be open from Spring 1995, but the entrance will be from Ralph Allen Drive. To keep the tranquillity of the estate, there will be no car park, except a small area for the disabled.

In medieval times the Prior of Bath had had his country seat in Widcombe, hence the name *Prior Park*. By 1730, Ralph Allen owned the estate and decided to build a grand house designed by John Wood as a glorious example of the possibilities of Bath Stone. Unhappily, Wood and Allen did not see eye to eye over the plans, especially the internal features. Wood saw the house as a chance to build a masterpiece, unfettered by constraints of finance, but Allen was a canny Celt, always looking for ways to cut expenses. Thus by the time the grounds were laid out in the 1750s, Wood had virtually disassociated himself from the project, and it was Richard Jones, Allen's Clerk of Works, who constructed the *Palladian Bridge*, which you can see from this vantage point. Almost certainly Allen was influenced by the one at Stowe. Alexander Pope was a frequent visitor to both houses, and as a noted landscape garden designer, his recommendations to Allen carried some weight. In its turn, the bridge at Stowe is probably a copy of the one at Wilton, but neither has the superb setting of this one. When it is fully restored, and the water once again cascades from under its arches, it will be worth the climb up Ralph Allen Drive to see it close to, from above as well as below. There is a sketch by Thomas Robins showing a long cascade, rather like that at Chatsworth, coming centrally down the slopes above the bridge, but it is thought that this may be a suggestion rather than something actually carried out.

Now turn back and begin to retrace your steps, but quite soon, on the left-hand side just by the end of the gardens of the house called *The Dell*, you will notice a footpath, down which you should wander. As you walk down here you can see the dovecote in the grounds of *Manor Farm* and admire the beautiful grouping of the manor and church. Further down the path you catch a glimpse of *Crowe Hall*, on the hillside, among trees. Amazingly, not only are you merely a mile from the centre of a busy city, but you are looking in *towards* that city. Bathonians are fortunate in having these oases of peace so near at hand. Unfortunately, traffic is always a consideration, and when you get to the end of the footpath, you must exercise great care in crossing the road. Turn left, noticing *Yew Cottages* on your right: they date from the 17th century. At the end of the street you will come to Ralph Allen Drive, with the gate-house on your left. This delightful lodge, with its charming Venetian window, is by John Wood, and was an indication to the visitor to Prior Park that he was nearly there. There were pillars on each side of the road, which was very much narrower. It climbs up to Combe Down in a series of straight stretches with easy bends between them, for it was not just the carriage road up to the house. A tramway ran down it, bringing stone down to the river from the quarries above. The quarries were mainly subterranean, and are now giving problems as modern traffic and houses put strains on the columns of stone that were left to hold up the roof. The tramway used gravity for the downward trip, with a brakeman riding rather precariously on the back of each truck. Once at the bottom and the stone unloaded, the empty wagons were pulled by a horse back up to the top.

Cross the road with great care to the gates on the other side. These lead to the cemetery of *Bath Abbey*, this side of Bath having become a popular area for burial grounds during the 19th century. This one was consecrated in 1844. The number of bodies beneath the floor of the *Abbey* and the monuments on its walls "demanded a larger space and more becoming arrangement". This was true: even today the odd bone can fall out from the floor into the channels which carry the heating. The cemetery was one of three landscaped by the famous gardener, architect, and reformer, John Claudius Loudon, who had become concerned about the lack of scientific principles in managing burial grounds. Such was his enthusiasm that he came to Bath despite the fact that his wife could see that he was dying. His death occurred as the work was completed at the end of 1843. He was just 60. During its creation it was found that the Romans had used this area for the same purpose, coffins, skeletons and coins all being found. Turn down the hill, cross the street called Perrymead and take the next left into

91

Prior Park and the Tramway, with trucks travelling down to Widcombe. From a print by Anthony Walker, c. 1754

Lyncombe Vale. In the 18th century there were two, possibly three, attractions which could be found in this area. The first was immediately on the corner, on the right-hand side of the road, and was Wicksteed's Machine, or the Bagatelle. We shall look at this one in more detail later, as we return. Another, Lyncombe Spa, we shall meet quite soon, when we shall discuss the possible existence of the third, King James' Palace. You will soon find a stream running along beside the pavement, the Lyn brook. Some of the springs which supply it caused the creation of the spa; it then was used to create ornamental lakes as well as supplying the power for two mills.

It is tempting just to wander along here enjoying the peace and quiet, but on your left you will eventually discover *Lyncombe Farm*. For most of its history this area must have been very rural; this farm seems to appear on Thorpe's map of 1742. Again on your left, you will next see a Victorian gate-house, with rustic trees and branches holding up the roof and porch, built when this became the entrance to *Lyncombe House*, now The Paragon School, but originally Lyncombe Spa. To see the house from the road, you should walk along beside the wall, past the old stable block, until you finally reach some gates from where you can see the school. We know from John Wood's account that in 1737 Charles Milsom had leased a fishpond, and while repairing a leak in it, he found a spring with what Wood calls "a strong sulphurous Smell". This and other symptoms led Milsom to believe this was a mineral spa. He then made the interesting discovery that the water would turn brandy dark purple. After a jollification, at which this peculiarity caused great mirth and excitement, Milsom associated with a Dr. Hillary and the owner of the ground (Wood does not name him, but the deeds make clear that it was one John Hickes) to promote the spa. Wood offered a design to cover the spring, which the collaborators refused, preferring one of their own. According to Wood (who not unnaturally is quite gleeful about it) the spring was ruined because the edifice was too heavy for the ground. What happened next is not quite clear, but by 1742, Milsom is no longer in the picture, and the other two had entered into a legal partnership to add a well-house to the present house, which they had already completed, and run it as a lodging house, spa, and recuperative centre. Hillary published a book about the waters which makes fascinating reading. He gives a description of the springs, and lists some of the cures. One is of a young girl who is clearly suffering from an eating disorder like anorexia; needless to say Lyncomb Spaw, as it was known, cured her completely.

Sad to say, the spa was not a success. Despite extensive facilities, including a coffee house and luxurious apartments, the partners eventually fell out in 1767, Hickes selling his share over the head of Hillary, who was reluctantly forced to come to an agreement. It was then run as an isolation hospital by Skeet and Kinnear. By the 19th century it was a private house, and was eventually acquired by George Moger, one of the family already mentioned in 'The Ups and Downs of Lansdown'. Leaving the family farm in Woolverton, George's father, also George, set up as a linen-draper, but moved into banking. The family became active on the City Council, and in 1857 George evidently felt this was just the place for a citizen of importance. It must have been a delightful home. Stop and listen carefully. The sound of water provides constant background music. You will notice there is water running under the gates and more coming through the wall. There are, as Hillary says, two distinct springs, one which covers the stones with a black residue, and one which leaves an ochre-coloured deposit. He says the temperature is 52°F: it still is. However, the springs are as temperamental today as they were then, causing problems for the school's groundsman. The water flowing under the gate has a discon-certing habit of rising in different parts of the garden, and you will notice that the other, coming out of the wall, has several exit points to choose from. There is one water-course directly underneath the house.

It is really thanks to the Mogers that the springs still run. Attached to the house was a cold bath house, dating from at least 1805 and utilising the springs. Members of the family used it regularly, and they must have been dismayed when the Somerset and Dorset Railway, granted powers to seize such ground as it needed, announced in 1872 it was coming through the grounds. Its activities, including tunnelling and embanking, had already cut off springs in other parts of Bath. The S&D issued a high-handed notice to the effect that it would pay £1600, which included "the amount of compensation for all damage and injury". It had reckoned without George Moger. The struggle lasted five years, at the end of which time, the Company had to agree to: allow Moger to keep the deeds; pay £1900 compensation, and *in addition*, build footbridges to the grounds on the other side; maintain an ornamental plantation on the slope facing the house; and "if any springs of water which was rising or being on the lands of the said George Moger ... previously to the works executed by the said Company are or shall be interfered with by the said works, the said Company shall and will lay down pipes to carry the water in pipes to the nearest channel for the same that existed previously to the said works having been executed". Moger was clearly a remarkable and determined man.

There is rather a mystery over King James' Palace. For a long time it was thought that this was another name for the spa, but the latest theory is that it was an extension to it, on the opposite side of the road. It was a public-house, tea garden, nursery with greenhouses – and gambling den! The confusion between the two occurs as early as 1779, but the mention of greenhouses has always meant that the north side of the road was a more likely position, the grounds of *Lyncombe House* being rather shady. On the other hand, we know the spa had gardens, for Thomas Robins made a sketch of them. The grounds of King James' Palace are described as a garden of pure delight, but by 1790 it was going out of fashion, and was available to let by 1792. It is last mentioned in 1805, when it was offered for sale. If it did have a separate existence, it has certainly vanished now. What is more interesting is the name. There is a local legend that following the abdication of James II, he hid in this part of the country, but this is extremely unlikely. However, his wife Mary of Modena visited Bath in 1687, and it is possible that she preferred to stay in the peaceful surroundings of Lyncombe than the bustling, noisy city. It is all conjecture: no definite reason can be given. This side of the road is also well-watered; look at the base of the wall and you will see holes to allow flood water from the stream to escape. If you walk a little further up the lane you will come to the gates of *Brookside Lodge* and *Hillbrook House*. With these names, you will not be surprised to see the stream in their gardens. Eventually it all joins up to form the water-course you have already met.

Looking up between these two modern houses you will see an 18th-century dwelling now called *Lyncombe Court*. Once called 'The Cottage', some research done for the Moger family indicates that

Milsom, having quitted the spa enterprise, bought a piece of land here called 'Mountain Close' and built this house, which his son Charles subsequently sold in 1774. It acquired the appellation of Cottage in 1871 when it was sold to Frederick Falkner. Return to the school, from where you will see the road fork, the left-hand path going up the hill. On the hillside is a house with six Venetian windows. This is *Lyncombe Hall*, a house which it is thought occurs on Thorpe's Map as Mr. Chapman's House. We have already met the Chapmans, and this sizeable property of early date would have been suitable for a family of their standing. There is supposed to be an odd connection with Queen Square in the garden of this house. About 1780, the balustrade, which is said to have enclosed the garden of the square, was removed and brought here to decorate the garden wall. Neglect caused its removal, but a piece is still said to be visible from here.

We must now leave this quiet valley and take the old road out, for Lyncombe Vale is not on Thorpe's Map of 1742, and although it certainly existed by 1786, as late as 1766 the Reverend John Penrose, visiting friends at the spa, describes the route as "an uphill and downhill, very rugged and uneven". Take the fork up to the left. You will shortly pass *Lyncombe Hall* on your right. Its street façade is now rather austere; a later addition has blotted out more Venetian windows on this side. Just beyond the Hall was the Unitarian Burial Ground, presented to the sect in 1819 by a Mr Howse, one time Chamberlain of the City (Unitarians were extremely active on the Council). One of the first to be buried there was Mr Howse's gardener, who had been a model for Thomas Barker's painting, *The Woodman*. The ground was eventually cleared, and the owner of the new property on the site must have had a grim sense of humour: he named it *Yorick House*. Continue to climb, watching for those glimpses of the views that have always fascinated visitors to this valley. See if you can spot the old gatepost of *Rosemount Farm*. Clearly the drivers of farm carts were not always very careful – and who was WB, who was so anxious to be remembered by later generations? At last you will see a house called *Rosemount* on your right, on the corner of Rosemount Lane, an improvement on its old but accurate name of Rough Hill.

Turn down the lane, once again admiring another aspect of this valley. Just down on your left is *De Montalt Cottage*, called after Earl de Montalt who inherited *Prior Park* in 1796. He was something of a philanthropist, founding the De Montalt Paper Mills, where Bank of England notes were made, and restoring the cottages in Combe Down which he hoped could be used as lodging houses for those recuperating after treatment at the hot springs. As you reach the bottom look to your left. Not only will you see the cliff of Widcombe Crescent, but you will also see the grounds of a house on the corner. This is now called *Bagatelle House*, a rather presumptuous claim since it is merely on the site of part of a group of buildings associated with the Bagatelle. The grounds belonged to the pleasure gardens which opened about 1740 and were at first called Cupid's Garden. An iron-bearing (or chalybeate) spring was discovered by Mr Wicksteed, a cameo engraver of Bath. Once again John Wood offered designs to cover the spring "every Way suitable to the Taste and Spirit of our Artist; but a Proposal by his Engineer, and others, to erect it with common Wall Stone to be first Plaistered, and Painted to imitate Brickwork, was such an Instance of Whim and Caprice, that when I got the Draughts I had made into my Possession, I never parted with them again". Wood was singularly unlucky with his efforts to enhance a spring, but he did tend to ignore financial limitations. The cold water spa seems to have been unsuccessful, and so Wicksteed promoted it as a pleasure ground, gaming house, and shop for his cameos and seals. It eventually became known as Villa Bagatelle, from the shape of the house, whose ground plan was like that of a bagatelle board. This was due to the alcove where the pump stood, and it was this mechanism which gave the place its other possible name of Wicksteed's Machine. He seems to have leased land from the Bennets, for there was access under the tramway to the lakes and walks in the manor grounds. A tunnel under the road was found during road-widening in the 1960s. Lyncombe Spa, with its air of greater respectability, seems to have been too great a rival, and Wicksteed sold out in 1773. The name was clearly too frivolous for Victorian owners, who called it Wilton or *Welton Lodge*. Turn left into Lyncombe Vale, and you will see the house on the corner with Ralph Allen Drive. It still has a semi-circular end.

Turn left and walk down the hill until you are outside *Ashley Lodge*. Look across the road to the garage. This looks unpromising as a site of historical interest, but proves how much of history can be hidden away. In amongst the modern accretions is an old stone building, which was, even in living memory, a flour mill. In its original state it was a very handsome building, and the owners believe that it may have been designed by Wood himself. If that seems fanciful, look at the Venetian window at the end; you have seen one identical with that on the lodge house just up the road. Furthermore, *Prior Park* itself has one, slightly grander but of striking similarity, at its east end. Allen was connected by marriage with the Bennets, and they collaborated to embellish the natural features of the valley. The building is dated at sometime in the early 1730s, just the very time when Wood was working for Allen, Behind the mill, the Lyn brook, having been brought under the road, was channelled into making the cascade which you saw from *Widcombe Church*, which in its turn fed three ornamental lakes. The lowest of these was the mill-pond, and the remains of a complicated sluice system still exist in the undergrowth at the back. It was probably a method of using the water as economically as possible, for the mill always had problems with its water supplies, even though the brook from *Prior Park* also flowed into the lakes. As the stream flowed from lake to lake, it was crossed by Chinoiserie bridges.

The mill was called Upper Widcombe Mill and was also used as a razor mill, i.e. where the stones were used for sharpening tools. The water came through the sluices and turned a water wheel, the housing of which is now used as a stairway in the garage. From there the stream returned under the road and ran down to Widcombe. The front door of the mill was quite grand and had steps up to it, allowing carts to back up to it to be loaded. The roof, like that of the Perrymead lodge, was stone-tiled. The miller and his family lived in the cottages still to be seen behind a wall, over to the east of the garage, and there were pig-sties and stables around the mill itself. There had been a mill here since the Middle Ages; investigations made during recent alterations uncovered old walls of Cotswold stone, and caverns hidden at the back. Their presence, and the alternative name of Deadmill, have led some to wonder if this is the site of the Dead-House or Plague-House, where those sick of fevers would be brought, to be cared for until their death.

Yet the site may be of even earlier occupation. During the flash floods of 1963, a rush of water caused the concrete in the yard to tip up and subside. A water course ran beneath, which at first was thought to be the stream crossing the road, until it was noticed that the water was flowing in the wrong direction. The stone-work of this drain was examined, and was considered to be of possible Roman date, although its purpose is not known. Coming forward in time, the mill became a garage in 1929, when the then owner of the manor, Sir Roper Wright, gave it to his chauffeur as a kind of redundancy payment. It has remained a garage ever since, except for a break during the last war when it was commandeered by the Admiralty as workshops. It was during this period that much of the original character of the mill was unfortunately lost, as extensive internal alterations were made.

Further down on your side of the road are two gate posts, which once led up to *Butt Ash Cottage*, now reached from Lyncombe Hill. Continue towards Widcombe, with a garden centre on your left. The planning committee sensibly turned down an application to build houses here, recognising the contribution such green spaces make to Bath's beauty. On the right is a pair of Victorian Gothic extravaganzas called *Oriel* and *Balliol Houses*, followed by a row of semi-detached cottages in what appears to be a Regency style. With their verandas and external shutters, which are probably original, they look as though they belong at the seaside. Eventually, on your left, after crossing the steep Forefield Rise, you will come to a Georgian terrace, in front of which the stream runs. Turn left to cross the brook and walk in front of this row, called Prior Park Buildings. They were built in 1825, almost certainly by John Pinch, in a severe style, devoid of almost all decoration except for the graceful balconies, whose design is picked up in the fanlights. This results in a composition of quiet elegance, enhanced by the presence of the stream, in whose clear waters you may see fish swimming. At the end you come to a steeply cobbled street with two very pretty cottages opposite, one called *Good Hope*. A few years ago these were threatened with demolition, but have been magnificently restored. The cobbled street appears to have had its stones laid rather carelessly, but this is deliberate, to give the horses' hooves grip on the steep slope.

Cross the road, and take the footpath to the left of *Good Hope*. This takes you to the back of Allen's Row, cottages built by Ralph Allen to designs by John Wood for the masons preparing the stone for shipping down river. The millstream ran where you are walking. Eventually the path comes round to the left at the back of Widcombe Terrace. On your left is a modern development, Armes Court, built on the site of the Poor House. It dated from 1777, but was demolished in 1961. The millstream flowed along here to a millpond, the site of which we shall see shortly, but before descending the steps to Claverton Street, you should realise that the last part of Widcombe Terrace is modern, a thoughtful and timely addition to an area which had lost so much of interest to the demands of traffic. At the bottom of the steps turn left, and you will find a grassy space now adorned not inappropriately with public toilets, since this is the site of the millpond of Hancocks' Mill. The stream then joined the Avon. The presence of the pond made Claverton Street very narrow. There was no view across to the river; a mass of houses filled the space. It included the Cold Bath, built by Greenway in 1704 as a cold water spa which came to be recommended by Dr. Oliver as an additional treatment to taking the hot waters. Wood tells us that the bathers were treated with "Respect and Civility". By this century it was falling into disrepair. Although architecturally a fine building, it was demolished when Rossiter Road was created. The sacrifice of Widcombe's houses to the needs of traffic began as early as 1825, with further losses in 1852. Turn back along Widcombe Terrace, which gives you some idea of the busy, populous area this once was. It was also rather lawless. Until 1835 the parish had no police force at all, and Holloway, the steep hill that climbed up from the south end of the Old Bridge, had become home to a criminal fraternity. There were frequent disturbances in the area.

Stop at the corner of Prior Park Road to look at the *White Hart Inn*. The inn dates from before 1733, but the sign above the door, although old, only arrived here after 1870, when the *White Hart* in Stall Street was demolished. Two paintings prove this assertion. One, in the possession of the Council, shows this beast over the door of the one in the city, and an 1860s watercolour has this pub without a sign. The animal also took a trip to an exhibition in America in the 1890s. You are now standing by Allen's Row. The tramway crossed the road here, continuing down to the river where the stone was loaded using Mr. Padmore's crane. The whole process became something of a tourist attraction, it being regarded as a very ingenious contraption. It was probably exciting rather than ingenious for the brakeman. It was dismantled about 1764, due, we are told, to the improved state of the roads. This explains why Penrose does not mention it, although he does comment on the crane. Prior Park Road continued to be private until 1921 when it was acquired by the city. When the carriage road was first built there was a gate across at the *White Hart*, and Mowbray Green,

Ralph Allen's Tramway and Mr Padmore's Crane. From A Prospect of Bath, by the Buck Brothers, 1734

writing in 1904, suggested that the house which once stood behind the inn was the lowest lodge. Harcourt Masters' map of 1803 actually calls the street 'Prior Park Gate'.

Cross to the other side, turn right and look up at the roof of the chapel, where you can see part of the texts. In 1961, following a re-roofing, the church elders had to apply for planning permission to reinstate them. A fine controversy ensued but the texts were replaced, using more modern language. Continue towards the canal, and as you turn the corner to take the footpath down to the canal, look above the doorway. This bears another text: "In the place of the thorn shall come up the fir tree", a reference to the replacement of the *Canal Tavern* in 1910 with the chapel's schoolroom! Now walk down to the canal, turn left, and then right over the bridge where the canal meets the river, to return to the city. The river path offers you some final charming prospects, of *Pulteney Bridge*, and of the *Abbey*, which so many years ago had owned much of the Widcombe Valley that you have just explored.

The Map's Right – Only The Buildings Have Changed!

Ask most people to imagine Bath in the 18th century, and they will probably visualise a city that includes elements from throughout the period; above all, they will tend to think of the layout of the city as we know it now. In fact, some of the best-known show-pieces, such as Royal Crescent and Great Pulteney Street, were built quite late in the period. The best way to observe the growth is by using contemporary maps. They must, however, be used with a certain amount of caution. They are not always reliable. Some have faults of scale and others include streets that were never built and miss changes that did occur. This walk attempts to find a route through Bath using a map of about 1750, but sometimes it proves necessary to go as late as 1789, while discovering some streets known in the 17th century. To make it easy for you, and to preserve one or two surprises, the map has been divided into 'bite-sized' sections; the original is surrounded by information about the city, and the key to the letters which indicate various places of importance. At the end you will find some comments on using maps for research. You may like to read them first, but en route we shall pass somewhere that existed in 1750 which you may find a pleasant place to take a break from walking and do some reading instead.

Start: We start at the East End of *Bath Abbey*, facing the Orange Grove. Ideally, we should have started at the West Door, but at the end it will be explained why this was not possible. Look at Map 1 and you will see that the row of shops to your right existed in 1750. Then they had plain gabled fronts and looked out over a grove of trees, in a rather more enclosed space than that to which we are now accustomed. Many of the shops had bow windows, to display to better advantage their variety of goods, which included such essential items as jewellery, lace, fans, shawls, and other knick-knacks. Some shops were known as toyshops, and sold articles like wedding rings, thimbles, and shoe-buckles as well as children's toys. At first many had hanging signs, used as advertising. They went out of fashion, for they looked untidy, and were a hazard in wet and windy weather, so in 1766 they were abolished. In front of them was a paved walk, of which the city was inordinately proud. From Abbey Church Yard to Terrace Walk, it was possible to visit all the shops without getting one's feet dirty or being splashed by passing traffic. On the far side of the grove from the *Abbey* was Nassau House, an early 18th-century residence with an extravagant display of ornaments and decoration. It survived until 1899, by which time it was a dye works. To each side of it were remaining sections of the city wall. Walk to the other end of the row of shops, and on reaching the end, you must turn right and imagine that you are passing under an archway, indicated by a small gap. It was *very* narrow, so if you

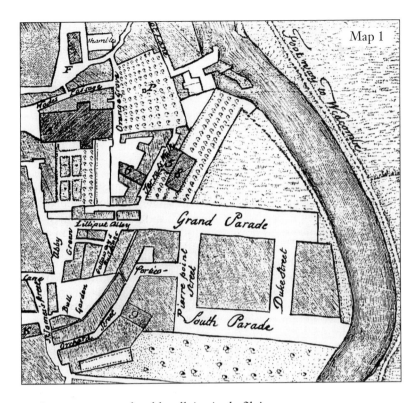

Map 1

are in a group, you should walk in single file!

You have now arrived in Terrace Walk; the second shop on your right was Leake's bookshop and circulating library. On your left would have been the entrance to the Lower Rooms, marked 5, with the newly built Long Room, marked 8. They burnt down in 1820, to be replaced by the Bath Royal and Literary Scientific Institute. This too was demolished in 1933, and public toilets (in the grand manner, it must be said) were put in their place. These have now been turned into a night club, but are remembered in the popular name for this triangle: 'Bog Island'. On your right, the shop fronts seem to have come forward, in line with Leake's shop-front. York Street was cut through in 1806, obliterating a second set of rooms designed by Wood, so when you pass down Terrace Walk you should ignore it (but not its traffic!). Eventually you arrive at *The Huntsman*, which by 1750 was The Parade Coffee House. The building was owned by the Ferry family, who had a silk mercer's shop at the first house in the Parade, where they sold "Rich brocaded SILKS in Gold, Silver and Silk. Flower'd Figur'd Strip'd and Plain SILKS of all sorts", such as "Padusoys, Tabbies Armozeens, Ducapes and Bumberzeens". You will notice that the Grand Parade, now North Parade, terminated at the river; the bridge and road are 19th-century. There was a pavement as wide as the one outside the *Compass Abbey*

101

Hotel all the way to the river bank. Here people could 'parade': simply walk up and down and admire each other.

To understand the ground plan of the next section, it is necessary to appreciate the changes that occurred in this area in the 1740s. The Assembly Rooms were built outside the line of the city wall, beyond which the ground was much lower, at the level of the present Parade Gardens. Within the wall, some levels were lower than modern ones, but were rising, partly due to the Georgian habit of building cellars, already explained in 'Street of Strangers'. When Wood built his Parades on the old Abbey Garden, he built them at an elevated level, lifting them well above the flood plain. This meant that they were higher than the old level of Lilliput Alley (now called North Parade Passage). If you look at Map 2, a plan drawn by Wood about 1749, not only will you see the narrow archway at C, and Leake's shop marked F, but you will notice steps down into Lilliput Alley, and steps from the narrow alley which led from Mr Allen's Garden. Gallaway's Buildings (North Parade Buildings) are missing, although they are present on the later 1750/1 map, when they were just being built. The whole street level was raised at about that time, but to avoid falling down imaginary steps, keep near the wall of North Parade as you turn right into Lilliput Alley and then left into Gallaway's Buildings.

Today you can escape from the southern end, but as you can see from Map 1, there was a wall right across, part of which still exists, to

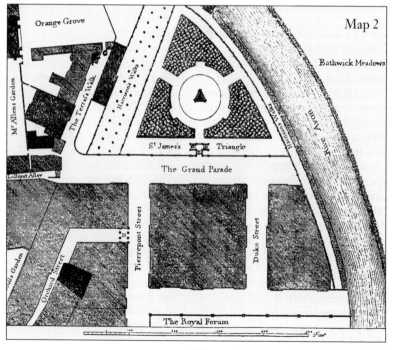

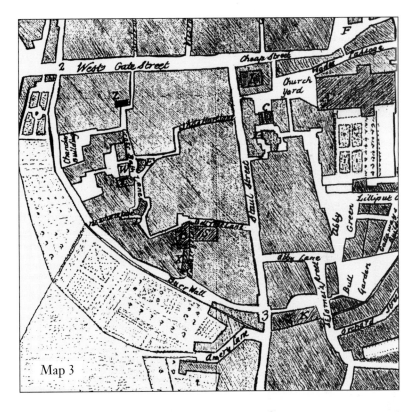

Map 3

separate it from what is usually called Bull's Garden. Wood (determined to be different, as usual) calls it Hull's Garden. The sharp angle at the top of the garden was caused by the junction with the city wall, of which a fragment survives in the loading yard for the modern shops to the south. Leave Gallaway's Buildings by the alleyway halfway along on the western side, bringing us into Abbey Green and on to Map 3. There are no houses shown on the north side of Abbey Green; but by the 1770 map, published by Leake, Abbey Street and Church Street have both appeared. They were all part of the development of the area by the Duke of Kingston in the 1750s, during which time the discovery was made of part of the Roman Baths. Although the north side has altered, the shape has changed little on the south side of the Green. By going under the archway to the left and turning right, we find ourselves in Abbey Lane, or Abbeygate Street as it is today. As you walk along you will notice that St James's Street has vanished under modern shops, and Swallow Street, on the right before the junction with Stall Street, has appeared. On arriving in Stall Street, we are on slightly precarious ground: road widening means the precise details of the buildings have changed, but the general shape is good enough to be acceptable. Turn left and then right into what your map calls Burr Wall, and today is Lower Borough Walls. We cannot, of course, see the South Gate, marked 3, which was removed shortly after this map was published. We shall now pay a visit to a very old street, but to get there, we have to use a map of 1789 (Map 4).

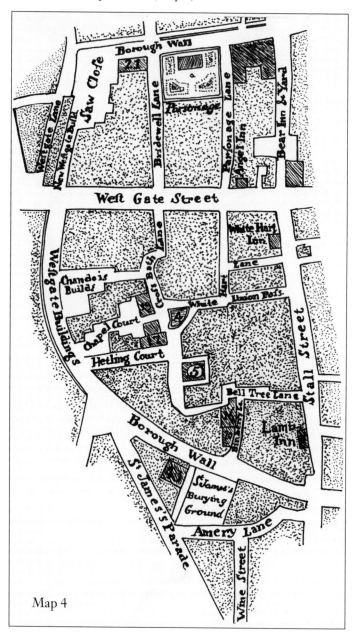

Map 4

Walk along Lower Borough Walls until you come to a little park on your left. Resist the temptation to cut diagonally across it; the map will not allow it. It was St James's Burying Ground, and was just outside the city wall. That is why we cannot use our map of 1750: the wall was in the way. At the far side is a footpath to St James's Parade, and as you walk down there, you will notice a chapel on your right, which is also marked on your map. There was originally a Roman Catholic chapel here, but just as it was about to be dedicated in 1780, it was burnt down, a victim of the Gordon Riots. The Catholics moved to Corn Street, and an Independent Chapel came here, to be replaced by the Quakers, who moved from a tiny meeting house in Cock Lane (Union Passage). When they moved out, the Methodists moved in; until 1994 it was a printing works. At the end of the footpath, turn left, and almost immediately left again down Amery Lane. It is now a dead end, although Wine Street comes up to meet it, yet it goes back to the beginning of the 17th century. Savile's Map shows a path bending round an enclosed area, with a small circular building, perhaps a dovecote, inside. By the end of the century it is quite definitely a lane lined with houses. The entrance was in Southgate Street, but during the 19th century the route was changed to come out in Lower Borough Walls. Wine Street appears on a map of 1770. Today, all the original buildings have gone, although there are indications of old walls, but the street, *literally* the street, survives. It was never of any importance yet it has remained while in other parts of Bath whole swathes of buildings have been swept away to create new roads.

Return to Lower Borough Walls by exactly the same route and cross the road to confront another problem. Just to your right is a narrow passage, Bilbury Lane, though it should properly be Binberry Lane. This is on Map 3, but leads to a winding lane called Bell Tree Lane, which no longer exists. Its claim to fame is that the Gunpowder Plot conspirators met there, in Bell Tree House, during August 1605. It was straightened out as part of the late 18th-century redevelopment of the area and was rechristened Beau Street, so even our 1789 map is no use, although the act to allow these changes was passed in that year. Hot Bath Street, which we find if we continue to walk westwards along the Borough Walls, is similarly out of bounds. On Map 3 you will see Nowhere Lane, so how about that? Well, it is there but no longer usable. If you walk past the shops on the corner of Hot Bath Street, you find a grassy gap between them and an old building known as *Abbey Church House*. This was once Nowhere Lane, which Wood tells us derived its name "from a Servant of the then Mayor, Mr. *Robert Chapman*, who was used to loiter away her Time in Gossipping in it; and as often as she was chastised for staying out, she as often insisted that she had been *No where*: But, at Length her Haunt was discovered, and then the Lane was called by the Name she had so often given it." Even if it were still open, it brought us out to the old Hot Bath, with the adjoining Lepers' Bath, which was altered and moved to one side in

1776–8 by John Wood the Younger. We could, therefore, have used a map of 1779, which has this change on it, but for reasons that will become apparent in a moment, we will stay with our map 4 of 1789. Continue past *Abbey Church House* and you will find a passage immediately on the other side of it, marked on Map 4 as Hetling Court, a name by which it is still known today. Walk to the end of it and stop. To your right, on the other side of the road, is the *Hot Bath*, which we know is all right for 1789, but there is a bit of a problem to the left, namely the *Cross Bath*.

The *Cross Bath* as we see it today was built in 1784 by Baldwin, but its serpentine front, which now looks down Bath Street, looked North at what was, at the time of building, some old houses. When Palmer built Bath Street in 1791–4, he turned the *Cross Bath* round, to give an attractive finish to the street. What is odd is that Taylor and Meyler, publishers of the 1789 map, seem to have made no alteration of the plan of the *Cross Bath* to allow for Baldwin's rebuilding. Perhaps they just forgot, or perhaps they considered that the shape was insufficiently changed to bother about it. This is likely, for at the time the work took place the site was so cramped that Baldwin had no option but to plan a bath that was almost identical in size with the old one, if not in design. It is possible, therefore, that he let his grand front look at a wall because he had no choice, not at that time knowing that there were going to be plans to change the area. However, had Nash Street been built, the front would have looked out into Westgate Street, and it is possible that Baldwin had that in mind. Fortunately it was not, and we can return to Map 3 to take us to Westgate Street. Turn left from Hetling Court, taking us past T and W on Map 3. These are *St. John's Chapel* and *St. John's Hospital*. This takes us up to Z, which was St. Michael's Chapel, but by 1750 a house for the Master of St. John's Hospital. The old chapel is remembered in the name St. Michael's Place. The bends to right and left are still there, and we can follow this lane to Westgate Street. Change now to the next section, Map 5. We are really going well here, with a clear run all the way up to Queen Square.

Cross Westgate Street into Bridewell Lane, which Wood insisted on calling Spurrier's Lane. It is certainly called that on Savile's Map, but it had changed by Gilmore's Map of 1692, with the building of a Bridewell or prison at the far end. That disappeared by 1711, to be replaced by a more kindly institution, the Bluecoat School. At the top of Bridewell Lane you still have the buildings of the school on your left, although these date from the 19th century, and the school has gone. To your right, according to the map, is a garden. This was the garden of Rectory House, which was once the vicarage of St. Mary de Staules church; the lane on the other side is called Parsonage or Vicarage Lane. When Elizabeth I said that *Bath Abbey* was to be the parish church of the city, the other parish churches were closed down, and the new Rector, Sir Richard Meredith, was invited by the Council to use this pleasant house as the Rectory. There was a catch. In return, he was to

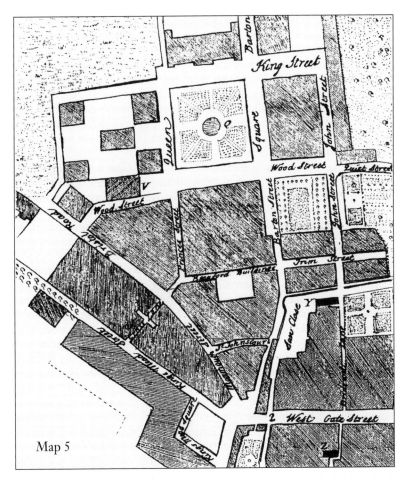

Map 5

allow the Council the use of the Abbey property around the church itself. We shall see the effect of that later. Sometime between 1779 and 1789, the Rectory was rebuilt in the garden itself, as you can see by looking at Map 4. It was a most impressive building but it lasted less than 80 years. It was demolished in 1858, and replaced by the extension to the *Mineral Water Hospital*. Cross the street, where, according to your map, you should meet a piece of the city wall. This has gone, but the street ahead of you is called Trim Bridge, referring to the archway over Barton or Berton Lane, the narrow passageway which ran in front of the houses at the base of the wall. By crossing the bridge and descending the slope, you ended up, as you do today, in Trim Street. This was one of the first streets to be built outside the city wall, and some of the houses are part of this original expansion. Opposite is the arch which is often now called Trim Bridge; go under it and find yourself in – John Street? According to the map you do, but today it is

107

called Queen Street. Although this name appears on maps from 1770 onwards, it does not always occur in the rate-books, and seems to have taken some time to become established. In 1750 it had only the first few houses on each sides, with gardens beyond. The first houses on your left appear to be the ones on your map, but those to your right, and the arch beneath which you walked, are more problematical. Are they the originals or a later rebuilding? However, there were certainly houses here in 1750, so if you decide refreshment is in order, *The Canary Cafe* is a pleasant place to take it, and perhaps read more about maps, their usefulness and their pitfalls.

Continuing up Queen Street from *The Canary Cafe*, imagine yourself passing the gardens on each side, so that you have an open view of Quiet Street which John Wood says that he named after "the meek Temper of a Washerwoman, espoused to one of the Builders". Alternatively, there is a local legend that Wood was trying to persuade the City Council to agree names for the streets. "What *are* we going to call them?" he protested, to which the councillors replied: "Quiet, John Wood!" If you look carefully you will see that you are indeed standing at the junction of Quiet Street, John Street and Wood Street. Sadly, there is no evidence whatsoever to back up this charming story; it is just something that *ought* to be true! Turn left away from Quiet Street along Wood Street, again visualising a garden to your left, before arriving in Queen Square. You will notice differences between today's square and the map. First of all, there was not a complete terrace on the western side, as we see now, but five buildings arranged roughly like the five spots on a dice. It was not, however, what Wood had really wanted. Having decided to create a square, he had planned a magnificent courtyard, with three plain but equal wings facing a grand palace (Wood's own word) on the northern side. Unfortunately, two wealthy lease-holders on the far side insisted on something grander, and Wood was forced into building what looked like three villas, two at each end and one set back. The infilling is by Pinch and dates from 1830. The garden was laid out far more formally than today, with flower-beds in each corner and a pond or basin in the middle, which contained the obelisk. That is still there, but in Wood's design, it went to a sharp point, which, he tells us, is the perfect shape for an obelisk. (By now you will have realised that Wood always knew better than anybody else on anything – or so he thought!) It was not, however, very practical, and fell during a storm. Wood tells us each of the four beds were planted with flowering shrubs enclosed by espaliers of Elm and Lime. This hid the ground floors (Wood calls them the basements) as you looked across the square, but not to the same extent as the present planting, dating from the 19th century. The diagonal walks were turfed, and the others were gravelled, the whole surrounded by a balustrade.

Pass along the south side of Queen Square, cross the little street (Princes Street) at the end, and you will be standing in Chapel Row. Several walks in this book have mentioned Wood's Chapel in the square, and by looking at the map you can see where it stood. Chapel Row, where you are standing, was virtually a footway. You will also notice that it is not called Chapel Row on the map; it was an extension of Wood Street. It was changed by 1766. We are now going to discover what has happened at the back of the west side of Queen Square, but since we cannot cross the road here without walking through the (imaginary) walls of the chapel, go down to the traffic lights and turn right there. Almost immediately on your right is a lane up which you should turn. It was called Stable Lane, but now calls itself Palace Yard Mews. This gives some clue to what those buildings must have been at the back of the square. Monmouth Street, off which this leads, was full of workshops and stables; indeed the whole city was full of stables, the modern equivalent being garages. In the 18th century they tended to put them at the back of developments, together with other offices such as brew-houses. Today there is no sign of the two blocks at the back of the square, which is hardly surprising, for they were altered late in the 18th century. Our Taylor and Meyler maps are not very helpful, for they tend to block in areas rather than show individual buildings or even gardens other than public ones. It is, however, still possible to get some idea of the grouping that Wood laid out, if the office car park on the right is open. Go through the archway, and by identifying the two surviving villas facing the square, you can begin to visualise the original plan.

Return to Stable Lane and continue to the major road at the top. Today this street is called Charlotte Street and is the A4; in 1750 you were looking at Barton Fields. We can, however, turn right and then cross to the north side of Queen Square. We shall not go up to Queen's Parade on which work did not begin until 1768. Our safest plan is to walk in front of the palace front, cross to King Street – and switch to Map 6! You are going to walk up the hill, the street now being called Gay Street, but on your map called Barton Street. When you get to the

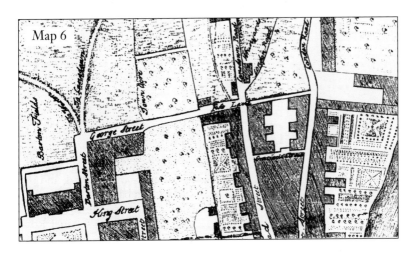

corner of George Street, it becomes obvious why. In our world of 1750 we cannot go up Gay Street to The Circus or Royal Crescent; not one of them exists. You are still looking at the Barton Fields, from which, at this junction, paths go off to Weston and Lansdown, then separate villages but now suburbs of Bath. Here we are, halfway through the 18th century, and you have reached the northern limit of the expansion at that time. Not only that, but our return route down Milsom Street does not exist either. A long field swept right down into the heart of the growing city, stopping at the old city wall. As stated in the introduction, one tends to imagine Georgian Bath springing into existence complete, like Minerva, to whom the Roman temple here was dedicated. In fact the Bath to which fashionable society flocked and over which Beau Nash reigned was a very small place, though growth was fast. In Smollett's book *Humphrey Clinker* a character describes the city as

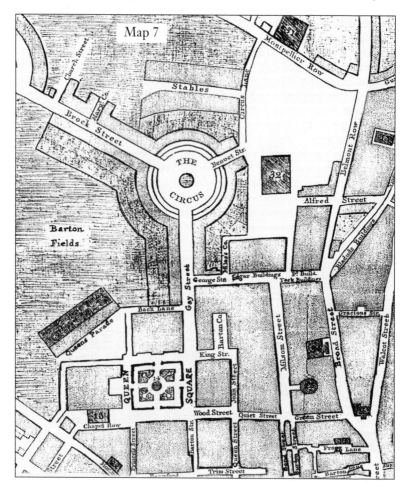

looking as though it had suffered an earthquake, because of all the incomplete houses.

Map 7, published in 1770, tells a different story. Now the Circus is complete, and Royal Crescent (disappearing out of the picture at top left) is shown as half built. It also indicates the *Assembly Rooms* (32); this was somewhat premature, for they were not open until the following year. By comparing Maps 6 and 7 and looking at buildings on each side of the road, especially Edgar Buildings, see if you can work out how the development fitted into the fields. You will shortly be turning down Milsom Street, but before you do, walk beyond it to the corner of Broad Street. By 1770 the road layout was that which we see now, but you will notice that in 1750 the London Road went across open fields, and a little lane called Foss Lane dropped down to Walcot Street, confusingly also labelled London Road. Foss Lane has totally vanished, but in Walcot Street there is a flight of steps, now leading only to the back of the *YMCA*, which could be a surviving piece of this old route. Return to Milsom Street, imagine yourself in the 1770s and walk down nearly to the bottom, taking the first turning on the left, Green Street. This avoids the problem presented at the bottom, where the first 'island' block between Burton Street and Bond Street shown on your map has been removed. This was a Georgian alteration as it occurred in 1810, but takes us out of the 18th century, as does the change from Frogg Lane to New Bond Street. It also means we can move on to our last map of the walk, Map 8, and back into 1750, although to return by any method other than using Trim Street does mean we are going to have to cheat a little. This is because great chunks of the city wall survived on this northern side, blocking our way through. Some disappeared with the building of Milsom Street, but going that way meant walking through the stable yard of *The Bear Inn*, no longer an easily definable route.

At the far end of Green Street you find yourself looking at *St. Michael's Church*. The shape on the map marked L is different from the present plan, but if you have already walked 'Street of Strangers', you know why! Turn right, the building on your right being the *Post Office*. This is modernish (1930s) but more or less on the line of the old street. The problem is New Bond Street, (1806) replacing the older Frogg Lane (all the maps are keen on the double 'g'). To be safe amid modern traffic you should use the pedestrian lights to cross to its other side. Imagine you have popped into a shop or two, to make allowance for turning slightly into the street. The next thing that would have happened is that Barton Lane should have appeared on your right, but it has gone. However, watch out for the two wooden doors just beyond the end of the colonnade which curves round from New Bond Street. The turning was about here. On the other side of the road Slippery Lane disappears down between some shops. Today it goes nowhere, but once it led down to the river. At the other end was the boatstall or moorings above the weir, and the ducking stool, which could be used for men as well as

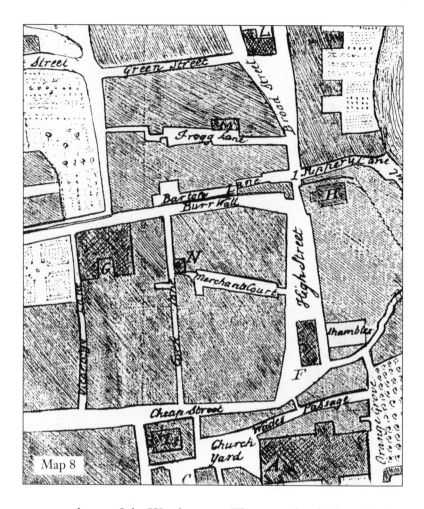

Map 8

women, whatever John Wood may say. There was also the ferry. Savile's Map has a delightful illustration of the ferry-man pulling the boat across the river using a rope fixed to each bank, a method that was still being practised at Bathampton as late as 1872. The lane joined up with Boat Stall or Fish Cross Lane coming down through the East Gate. That still survives at the back of the *Guildhall*, but the old lanes leading to it were obliterated in the 19th century. Imagine yourself passing under the North Gate (indicated by the figure 1), and cross Upper Borough Walls (or should that be Burr Wall?) on your right before turning to walk along it.

Now we are on safe ground all the way back to the *Abbey*. The alleyway now called Union Passage will shortly be on your left. On your map it is called Cock Lane, despite Wood's protestations that it should be Lock's Lane. Turn down here, and you will soon notice

Northumberland Place on your left. As far as one can make out, this is pretty well on the site of Marchant's Court (Merchant's, wrongly, on the map). The building marked N was the Quakers' Meeting House. There was no entrance from your right, but you will see on the map that there was a small court a little further down. This too seems to have survived. A few yards down, The Corridor, built in 1825, cuts across. Look how much narrower it is to your right than to your left. Is the section on the right the odd little lane which must once have been an entry to *The Bear Inn*? It seems to be in the correct place. Leaving this speculation, we continue down Union Passage/Cock Lane to Cheap Street. Here we look across the road and see an alley disappearing under an archway into Abbey Church Yard. This precise route goes back at least to about 1600, for Savile's Map shows exactly the same thing happening, although the building that forms the archway has changed since Savile's day. Cross, go under the arch, and turn left to face the *Abbey*.

Strictly speaking our walk has finished, but at the beginning it was said that we should have started here. Look at the map and you will see what prevented us: Wade's Passage. To follow its course we should have had to walk out into the centre of a busy road. These houses were the result of the deal made with the first Rector. From the mid 1500s onwards they were constructed by the Council, using the walls of the *Abbey* to reduce the cost of building. By the start of the 18th century they clung to the walls in such profusion that it was impossible to walk between the *Abbey* and High Street. Instead, as Wood tells us "the small Doors of the *Abbey Church* were left open, to make a Communication between the *Walks* and the *Pump*". In other words, the north aisle of the *Abbey* had become a footpath. In the 1720s people began to regard this as unseemly, and Field Marshal Wade, who lived at what is now the National Trust shop, provided the chief contribution towards the removal of some houses, creating a wider path. Nevertheless, most remained as busy little shops of all kinds: jewellers, greengrocers, haberdashers, and butchers, to name just a few. Further houses were attached to the south side, part of the development of the area by the Duke of Kingston. In 1823 the decision was taken to remove the clutter of shops and houses, but it took ten years to achieve, a delay caused by some leases still having years to run. At the end of that time, the Earl Manvers, descendant of the Kingston family, agreed to remove those on the south side as well, provided a carriage road was made from the terrace to the Parades. The Abbey walls were finally free of the encumbrances that had hidden them for nearly 300 years.

Finally, as promised, a word about **MAPS**.

Maps are among the most fascinating documents a researcher can use, but there are dangers. Thanks to the Ordnance Survey we have come to expect an extremely high standard of mapping in this country, but even OS maps can, and do, have errors. Early maps can be very variable. 17th-century maps, such as Savile's, Speed's, and Gilmore's, are not to scale, and try to be little pictures of cities, rather than true maps.

Recently it has become fashionable to produce tourist maps of Bath in the same style; though pretty, one wonders how easy they are to use. 18th-century maps sometimes show streets that were never built. There would have been an intention to build, but for a variety of reasons, it never happened. Wood's map of the city, published in 1735, has a circular building marked very clearly just outside the city wall, to the south-west. It never existed. It was Wood's proposal for what was to become the Mineral Water Hospital, but on a different site. He had planned an Imperial Gymnasium, where patients could take medicinal exercise, and use a supply of water piped there from the springs. Thanks to some double-dealing by his opponents, its only relic today is on his map. Later maps show the full extent of the proposed Pulteney estate in Bathwick; again, the scheme collapsed, this time due to bankruptcies caused by war with France. When using maps of this period, therefore, the information should always be checked against other evidence, such as a map drawn by another surveyor, or rate-books. (In fact this is a good rule to apply to *any* map, whatever its credentials!)

The best maps and plans, though somewhat limited in their scope, are those on deeds (where it is in everyone's interest to get the facts right) and surveys done for landowners or parishes. Harcourt Masters the architect was originally a surveyor who produced some excellent plans of the Rivers Gay Estate, and went on to create some fine maps of the city in the early 19th century. Another source of information are tithe maps, and their accompanying registers, drawn up around 1840 (a tithe was a rent or tax paid to the parish). Again, as legal documents in which money was involved, they tend to be accurate, and the registers list owners and occupiers. The finest map of the city, however, was produced in 1885–6 by the Ordnance Survey. Its scale was 1:500 or just over ten and a half feet (yes, feet) to the mile. It even pinpoints trees and paths in gardens. Although apparently of too late a date to be much use, in fact its fine detail and accurate surveying make it a marvellous template. It is possible to work out from it where previous maps are inaccurate, or show how housing developed on earlier estates and open ground. This can often be done by comparing field boundaries, which are surprisingly enduring.

If you feel you would like to look at more maps, your local reference library and city or county records offices will certainly have plenty for you to study, although you may have to use micro-film or photo-copies. They can bring hours of pleasure!

AND FINALLY...

Having completed the other walks in this book you probably feel that there is little you can now learn about the city. Are you sure of that? This walk asks the challenging question:

So You Think You Know Bath?

Despite having walked its streets and looked at its sights, you may be surprised at how many little details you have missed. Just to prove it, **start** by standing in Abbey Church Yard with your back to the West Front of the *Abbey* (no cheating by looking first!) This is smothered in detail and since three walks have begun or ended here, you should have noticed it. How much can you remember? Now turn and look. Most people recall the details featured in the dream of Oliver King, the bishop appointed by Henry VII. On seeing the Norman Cathedral looking shabby and worn (it *was* 400 years old), he received a message in a dream, commanding him to build a new church. He saw the Holy Trinity surrounded by angels, and a ladder with angels ascending and descending. A voice spoke, saying, "Let an OLIVE establish the crown, and a KING restore the church". Since his name was OLIVEr KING, he took this to be words from God, although whether God makes puns like this is a moot point. On the front, therefore, you can see Jesus riding in glory in the midst of what is now a flock of featureless lumps, but was once a flight of angels all leaning out and up to see Christ's face. Unfortunately weather and pollution have worn them away. John Wood loathed them; he described them as looking like "so many Bats clung against the Wall". Two ladders (Wood was upset about the addition of the second), each topped by a Godhead to complete the Trinity, lead from Heaven to Earth, with angels mainly ascending, but two, the third from the top on the left-hand side and the second from the top on the right are descending. They are *not*, as some think, fallen angels thrown out of Heaven; it is simply that it is difficult to show the difference between going up and down a ladder, so to make it plain, the Tudor stonemasons carved them coming down "partly flying, partly crawling, headforemost", as Wood has it. Needless to say, he did not like them either. At the base of each ladder is a figure which E.M.Hick, writing in 1913, identified as a shepherd. Oliver's name is on the Abbey in the form of a punning rebus. To each side is the carving of a tree, representing an olive tree, encircled by a crown (for King) and topped by a bishop's mitre (or hat).

There is, however, much more than that. On each side of the door are the patron saints, SS. Peter and Paul. Peter, to the left, is missing his halo, although Paul has his, looking rather like a coolie's hat; Peter has also shrunk somewhat. This is due to the fact that at some stage he has lost part of his head. Some think this was damage perpetrated by Roundhead soldiers during the occupation of the city in the Civil War,

115

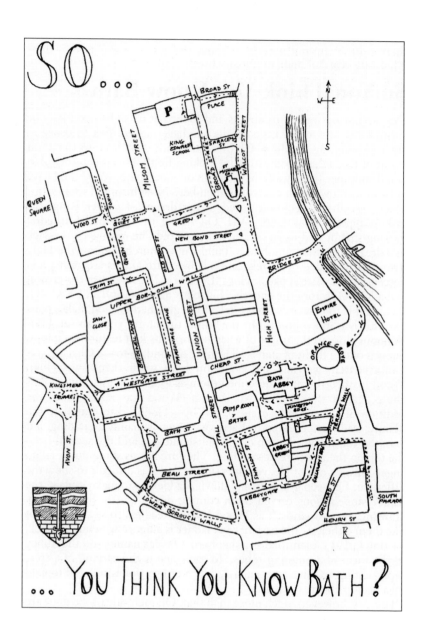

SO...

... YOU THINK YOU KNOW BATH?

while modern Parliamentarian supporters deny it. One can only say that if no attempt was made to destroy the decorations on the church at this time, then Bath was uniquely lucky. Whatever the cause, efforts to restore the head proved ineffective, and a new head was carved out of his old beard. There are those who say that these are not the patron saints, but a Bishop and a Prior. This ignores the presence of the halo, and the faded inscriptions on the plinths, which we know from a report of 1798 positively identify these as Peter and Paul. The royal connection is established by the presence of Henry VII over the door (although this is a comparatively recent replacement). He stands over his own coat of arms, supported by a Welsh dragon and a greyhound, and Christ sits over the Tudor Rose supported by two greyhounds. They, in turn, surmount the arms of Bath Abbey and the diocese, and below them again, in the window itself, is a large bird. Hick describes this as an angel with a shield, and judging by (admittedly rather murky) old photographs, it does seem to have changed its appearance during the postwar restoration. It is now said to be the eagle of St John, but it really looks more like a monster pigeon. Perhaps it is the dove of peace. The Tudor Rose occurs once more; can you find it? To give you a clue, it is down low, and is matched on the other side with a portcullis.

Until the most recent restoration, it was thought that the statues on each side of the ladders were the twelve apostles, but it is now suggested that one is the Virgin Mary, and another, with the bare knee, is John the Baptist. The other ten are the remaining apostles after the exclusion of Judas Iscariot, and St. Peter, who is already on the front. Some have identifying marks, such as St. Andrew with his cross. St. Philip, up on the top left-hand side, was so badly damaged due to a fault in the stone that he has had to be recarved. These figures were sculpted as if they were real people standing in elevated positions, with their hair and garments blowing in the breeze. There are two more statues, one over each of the side doors. That to the left holds a scroll and that to the right holds a money-bag. Since legal contracts were often enacted just within the church, it is possible that these indicate that to the left was where legal matters of the Parish not involving money took place, while the other porch was for matters involving payment of money. This would include marriages (the Wife of Bath had had five husbands at the church door). Alms were distributed to the poor from here. While looking at the doors, notice that the symbols of the passion are carved in the spandrels of all the doors. These are the crown of thorns and the five wounds, in the heart, hands and feet. This church was, of course, Roman Catholic before Henry VIII's break with Rome, and the dissolution of the monasteries. The West Doors were given in 1618 by Sir Henry Montagu, Lord Chief Justice to James I, to commemorate the repairs to the church by his brother, Bishop James Montagu. They are made of solid oak, and are decorated with shields associated with the Montagu family.

We have nearly finished with the West front, but you may notice, above the side windows, some words in faint relief. They say "Domus Mea … Domus Oronis": this is medieval shorthand for "My house is a house of prayer". It is said they were originally gilded. There are also some ribbons on each side of the ladder. The words on these have totally vanished, but it is thought that they were a quotation from Judges: The trees went forth on a time to anoint a king over them; and they said unto the olive tree, "Reign thou over us". If that is the case, one is forced to the inescapable conclusion that Oliver King was either a man with a pronounced sense of his own importance – or a mischievous sense of humour. We shall now see what else we can find on the other three sides of the church, but before leaving Abbey Church Yard, look across at the Pump Room. Beneath the triangular pediment you will see the Greek letters ΑΡΙΣΤΟΝ ΜΕΝ ὙΔΩΡ, which roughly translated means "Water is Best", an appropriate motto for a spa. You will see the words again, once in English and once in Greek. You are going to take Wade's Passage to leave the church yard: in case you have not done the map walk, it is the gap to the north of the church. Before doing so, notice the house on the corner, to the right of the National Trust shop. The Circus is celebrated for John Wood's use of the three classic orders of architecture: Doric, Ionic and Corinthian. Yet here they are on a much earlier building, though with pilasters (or flat columns) rather than pillars. Go through the passage to reach High Street, and in doing so you will see the statue of *Rebecca at the Well*, which has become (dare one say it?) a well-known meeting place in the city. But I wonder how many Bathonians know when it was erected and by whom. The plinth tells you: in 1861, by the Bath Temperance Association. Not surprisingly, it is here that we find the first repetition of "Water is Best", facing out towards the market-place – which was once lined with inns!

Turn back to the church. Here and there along the north wall you can find traces of the houses which clung to the wall, as described in 'The Map's Right', in the form of slanting marks left by the roofs. There are several on the corner of the transept. You will also notice that the *Abbey* has a kind of moat. This is the early 19th-century ground level; the Tudor level was slightly lower and the Norman level was lower again. This meant that when Abbey Church Yard was raised, there had to be steps down into the church. The floor was finally raised to meet the outside in the mid-19th century. Walk beyond the transept to the north-east corner of the *Abbey*. Look at the last window in the north wall. To its left you will see the remains of an archway included in the structure, as if there had been another window. This was not tidied up into the wall until the late 17th century, and can be seen hanging out of the end of the church in Savile's map. It was always thought that this was the remains of a Norman archway, for the Tudor builders utilised the walls, stone, and foundations of the old cathedral, but it is now believed that *Bath Abbey* had a Lady Chapel jutting out at the East End.

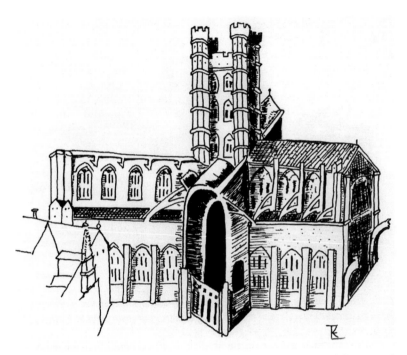

Bath Abbey from Savile's Map of 1600, showing arches jutting out of the east end, work still in progress on the transept, and the roof missing from the nave

Certainly Smith's 'Map' of Bath, published in 1588 but possibly drawn 20 years earlier, shows one. This map is really more of a sketch and is not desperately accurate, but so grand a church, especially a Priory, was likely to have one. After the Reformation it might well have been deemed unnecessary and demolished, particularly as at the end of the 16th century, the City Council was trying to lay its hands on as much of the Abbey property as it could. Go round the corner and look at the spandrels of the doorway. Here you will see the letters I.F. and a coat of arms with a fleur de lys. These are the initials and arms of Jeffery Flower, who paid for the end of the Abbey to be neatened and a doorway inserted. There are other early remnants to be seen here. Poking out of the base of the buttresses at each side of the East Window are the remains of pillars: again, it has always been said that they are Norman, but the recent theory means that they could be part of the Lady Chapel. It is the constant changes in theories that makes local history such an intellectually satisfying game. If you are bored with crosswords and jigsaws, and detective novels have lost their charm, combine the three and go in for historical research!

Before rounding the corner of the *Abbey*, you may like to ponder the name Orange Grove, which is where you are standing. There had been a grove of trees here from the 17th century, but the name Orange

Bath Abbey from Orange Grove before the 19th-century alterations. The houses in Wade's Passage can just be seen to the right of the Abbey. From a print by Nattes, 1805

comes from the presence of the obelisk. It was erected by Richard Nash to celebrate the visit of a Prince of Orange, who came to take the waters, and appropriately it is Alkmaar, Bath's twin town in Holland, which now supplies the spring bulbs for the garden. Now walk between the *Abbey* and the end of the shops on Orange Grove, noticing the side of these old buildings. Here you see the signs of their age, together with some blocked windows. Turn right into Kingston Buildings, and walk along until you reach the end of the South Transept. Here you will find a date: 1576. To explain this, it is necessary to give a very brief explanation of the very lengthy building of the *Abbey*. Begun in 1500, the nave and transepts were still incomplete when the dissolution of the monasteries took place in 1539. The church, which eventually arrived in the Council's hands, stood in this unfinished state, plundered occasionally for stone and lead, but Elizabeth I decided to take an interest in it, and she held a collection for it to be made usable, work beginning in 1576. (It was still in progress when Savile drew his map about 1600.) She also ensured that it would be used, by closing down all the parish churches within the walls. The Council allowed the rector, Sir Richard Meredith, to use the rectory of St. Mary de Staules, in return for handing over the leases of the land around the church. Thus it was that the houses grew up around it, the rents going into the City Purse.

Now look up at the reveal of the window, to the left-hand side. If you peer hard, you will see the date 1750, and about four sets of initials. These are masons' marks, left by some 18th-century workmen. Before moving out into the open space ahead of you, look up at the end of the houses facing the *Abbey*. You can see the name of the block, Kingston Buildings, but in phonetic spelling, a reminder that Sir Isaac Pitman, inventor of shorthand and developer of phonetics, had offices here. Walk out into the open space and notice the multitude of pinnacles that decorate the church. Many were not here until about 160 years ago, and such a furore was caused when they were added, it became known as 'The Pinnacle War', waged principally in the pages of the local paper. They were added at the same time as the flying buttresses were added to the nave. This part of the church had never acquired them because fan-vaulting, which exerts a sideways thrust, had never found its way to the nave, although it had been intended: there were little stumpy bits at the top. In 1833 G.P.Manners decided to make the Abbey 'look right' by adding them, together with the pinnacles which act as a counter-weight, directing sideways thrust downwards. Execrations and contempt were heaped on his head. The experts stated that the angle of the existing buttresses was such that they were not carrying any strain, so the whole lot were unnecessary. As it turned out, they were wrong. Manners added his buttresses, but as the old flat roof remained in the nave, he made them of light construction. In 1867, Gilbert Scott decided to put vaulting in the nave, and, probably being unwise enough to believe the experts, he did not strengthen Manners' handiwork. By the early 1900s the roof was pushing the church apart, and new, solid buttresses were put in place. Yet to this day you will hear people announce that they are fakes.

We have nearly finished with the *Abbey*; just a couple of points remain. The tower is rectangular, a relic of using the Norman foundations, which did not lie in the right place to allow the more usual square one. Incidentally, you may be unaware that the *Abbey* is a calendar. Not only are there 52 windows, one for each week of the year, but there are twelve normal-sized pillars inside, for the months, four large ones for the seasons, and (once upon a time) seven doors for the days of the week. Finally, walk up to the south-west corner. Here you will find a stone, carved in a quietly dignified style, commemorating the postwar restoration. Beneath it a new one has been added, as a reminder of the latest restoration, but in an odd script that one can only suppose represents the trendy attitudes of the modern Church of England. There is also a parish boundary mark, St.PPP, on the side of this buttress, because the parish of St. James's used to come right up to the *Abbey* walls.

At last we can leave the church, so walk south to York Street, turning slightly left. Between a shop and the large building in the Greek Revival style is a gate with a sign which says '*Ralph Allen's Town House*'. If it is open, and during office hours it should be, go through and down the steps. You will find yourself in a tiny courtyard which is almost overwhelmed by the magnificent building to your right. This was indeed Allen's house in the city, which by chance is a good example of how difficult it is to be an accurate guide to the city. Some architectural experts state categorically that it is *not* by Wood, others that it is

Ralph Allen's House in its original state. From a 19th-century water-colour by Henry Lansdown

definitely by him, and yet others, including Wood himself, are rather vague. Probably it is by him, but he regarded it as rather vulgar and thus, most unusually for him, does not brag about it. This is sad, for it is a dazzling piece of work in this tiny setting. It was actually an extension to the house which was facing you as you came into the courtyard, where Allen first lived and worked. This would have been 17th-century, like *Sally Lunn's*, but was refronted to match the new extension. The puzzle is, how did the houses join up? After Allen left for Widcombe, new properties encroached on it from the east, until it was left as the dark courtyard you see today. Go back up the steps and turn right into York Street, created in 1806. Immediately on your right is the aforementioned Greek Revival building, now the *Friends' Meeting House*, but built as the Freemasons' Hall and opened by Lord Newark in 1817. The architect was William Wilkins, and he must surely be responsible for the houses on the other side. This is one of the most disregarded pieces of architecture in the whole of Bath, but it really is a little gem. It provides a foil for the temple opposite, giving balance to this rather narrow street. It appears they were built as shops: the main windows all have shutter grooves at the top, and the door of No.13 has shutters in the door, now permanently fixed.

Continue to the end of York Street and turn right along Terrace Walk. On the side of *The Huntsman* you will see a sign to *Ralph Allen's House*. For many years this was the only vantage point from which to see it. It is still worth a quick trip down there, not only to get a less cramped view of the house, but also to look up at the roof of the *Friends' Meeting House*. Here you will see a lantern skylight, decorated with some attractive plasterwork garlands. Return to Terrace Walk, make your way eastwards in front of the *Compass Abbey Hotel*, and turn right, down Pierrepont Street, stopping at the corner of Henry Street. Look across the road, where you will see Wood's terrace, South Parade. It was here that he hoped to have his Grand Forum, a plan dismissed by the Council as "chimerical". In the early 19th century the scheme was revived, and maps show Kingston Square, with South Parade as its north side. It was never built, but the name was put up in readiness. You will see it on the wall behind you. Look back at the Pierrepont Street end of South Parade and up at the roof, just above the cornice, you will see some sections of balustrade. On the rest of the front it is missing, although the intervening pillars are still there at this end. There were also vases at each end; these too have gone. Return back along Pierrepont Street and notice the portico you pass on your left, now marked Pierrepont Place. There can be very few Bathonians who know that its real name is St. James's Portico, and that Wood's name for the present Parade Gardens was to be St. James's Triangle. Bath Festival has its offices down here, in a house on the left-hand side. It was once the home of the Linley family, aptly enough, for the whole family was musical, and in particular Elizabeth, who eventually married the playwright Sheridan. There were eight children all together, and for a while the nursemaid was one Emma Hart, better known to posterity as Lady Emma Hamilton. Coincidentally, at a later date Nelson stayed just across the street at No.2 Pierrepont Street.

Walk back in front of the *Compass Abbey Hotel* towards *The Huntsman*, go to the left of the pub down North Parade Passage and left again into North Parade Buildings (Gallaway's Buildings). Walk down it a short way before turning back to look at *Sally Lunn's*. Up in the gable is a hole, in which you will see a stone owl. In barns, round holes like this were made to encourage owls (hence 'barn owls') who were the farmer's friends in keeping down vermin. Whether or not such an aperture in a town house is an owl hole is debatable; to be fair, when this was built it was close to the city wall, with an orchard outside, and rodents were almost certainly a problem. Turn back and walk to the southern end of the terrace to look at the last house on the left-hand side. Here you will find some 18th-century graffiti:– IG 1774. Georgian vandals were set on making indelible reminders and nothing was sacred. *Sham Castle* and the *Palladian Bridge* are deeply scored with such unwanted engraving.

Go down the slope at the end of Gallaway's Buildings, keeping the old wall on your right. It is of very early date, being the southern limit of the monastery. As you turn to your right at the end, you will pass a fish restaurant (known locally as Fishy Evans) and in front of you will be the modern *St. Michael's Arch*. Notice on the wall of the restaurant an old hinge. The Abbey Gate stood here on this site, at right angles to the present arch, and this is its hinge. Beneath the arch is a brass plate with an edition of Speed's Map of 1612, on which you will be able to identify the wall and the Abbey Gate. Turn left along Abbeygate Street then right into Swallow Street. When the modern block was being constructed, the remains of the long-lost Bishop's Palace were found underneath, and to commemorate this, a replica of one of the carved stones is near the corner. One's first impression of Swallow Street is that it is rather tatty, but some of the double doors on the right-hand side have some fine iron hinges. Also on the right is a building with a chimney disguised as a fluted column; its doorway, slightly further on has the Bath coat of arms above it. Or has it? The accepted coat of arms of the city has a wall, representing the city wall, surmounted by water, thought to represent the river. But the 1623 arms, authorized by a Herald's Visitation in that year, had them the other way up. There is a set in the chancel roof of the Abbey. It was thought that it was a representation of the King's Bath. By looking closely at these you will see that the water is at the bottom. This clearly stamps it as the work of Major Davis, City Architect from 1862 until his death in 1902. Without telling anyone, he decided to reinstate the old arms on civic buildings, which he did on the *Guildhall*. There was the most enormous outcry (though one is at a loss to understand why) and Davis was forced to put back the 'accepted' arms. However he seems to have got away with it on the laundry, for that is what you are looking at, complete with the boiler-room and chimney.

From the end of Swallow Street you will be able to take a good look at part of York Street, noticing in particular the animals beneath the cornice at roof level. Can you find the wolf (or is it a bear?) holding a fish? You will have to step out into York Street to find it. In doing so you may notice what seems to be Punch's dog, Toby, wearing a ruff around his neck. The bridge, decorated with a fine carved head on each side, is another disguise, carrying a pipe over to the laundry! On the opposite side of the road from Swallow Street is another commemorative plaque, with some Greek writing you should recognise. Go westwards to Stall Street, turn left, and walk down to the cross roads, where you turn right along Lower Borough Walls. On the left-hand side you will see, next to the small shops, an unfinished Georgian block, with the fireplaces all ready for the next houses. Further along on the left, watch out for another row of shops which includes a fine glass shop sign for W.D.Lane's Dairy. There was also a butcher of this name in Widcombe; presumably the businesses were not unconnected. Turn right up Hot Bath Street, passing Beau Street on your right, and stand with your back to the *Cross Bath*, looking down the way you have come. Most people, especially those who have walked 'Labyrinths and Lace', have noticed the words 'Hetling Pump Room' on the building to your right, with the blocked doorway beneath a portico, but less often seen are some other words up high on the old Technical College Block, on the corner of Hot Bath Street and Beau Street. It was built in 1824 as the Royal United Hospitals, the uniting hospitals being the Bath City Infirmary and the Bath Casualty Hospital. The Albert wing, curving round into Hot Bath Street was added in 1850–60, and the words 'In Memory of Albert the Good' may *just* be seen, beneath a layer of grime, in the band at attic level.

Looking left, you will see a narrow house at the back of the *Hot Bath*, with two statues on it. Most locals should recognise these, although they will not know who they are or where they came from, because no-one is quite certain. It is possible that they came from the old town hall demolished in 1760, but where were they before that? All that is known is that they are very old, which is why they are here. This was the first Bath Museum, established in the early 19th century mainly to display the various Roman artefacts discovered about the city. There was another venerable statue on the side, but somehow it has been lost! The house itself is sometimes described as the smallest in Bath; it must be the narrowest. Finally look through the window into the *Cross Bath* itself. On one wall is a carving of Bladud, the legendary founder of Bath, and on another is a picture of the decorative Melfort Cross which stood in the bath from 1688 to 1784. Notice particularly the carved cherubs. Walk up the narrow path at the back of the bath, with the wall of St. John's Hospital on your left. Shortly before the lane on the left you may notice in the wall a decorative carving involving circles and links like a chain. One piece is rather weather-worn. Wood had always intended to put carvings from the old hospital on the face of the building; is this the only piece that found its way to the walls, or is it, as some locals believe, part of the Norman cathedral? Take this lane, between the Hospital and the Little Theatre, cross the road, turn right and then left across Avon Street into Kingsmead Square.

This was always rather more of a diamond than a square, and is now lacking one side. It was built on the King's Meadows by an architect called Strahan, whom John Wood loathed and detested. It was never very popular, and although Penrose, in 1766 and 1767, had friends staying there, they tried to avoid using Avon Street, "a Street of ill Fame" except for a visit to buy second-hand silks for dresses. Only one of the original houses in Avon Street still survives, at the corner of the square. It has a high doorstep, a necessary precaution when the river flooded. As described in 'A Transport of Delight', Penrose became involved in a fight with some local roughs at the West Gate, continuing in the square. The house at which his friends were staying is described as "the Corner-House in King's Mead Square, next King's Mead Street". It appears, therefore, that they were in *Rosewell House*, the elaborate building on the west side, which you should now examine. In an odd way, this house probably helped the area to decline, for it was in quite the wrong style. At a time when Palladian architecture was all the rage, someone, probably Strahan, designed this in the, by then, despised Baroque fashion. It has many delightful details which people pass everyday without noticing. The house derives its name from the builder, Thomas Rosewell, and, like Oliver King, he signed his name on it. Up at the top, in the segmental (arched) pediment, is the carving of a rose and a well, together with the date. All the windows are framed by highly decorated architraves with faces in the keystones, but the two central ones are really exuberant. The first-floor one, above the doorway, is flanked by grotesque male figures and has a fierce dog in the keystone, while the window above that is a joyful flourish of swirls and whorls and foliage. Now go back to the east side of the square, and cross the double junction into Westgate Street.

As you walk along the street, notice on your right *The Grapes*. Not only is this an extremely old name for a pub, for Roman taverns had bunches of grapes hung outside, but the building is also of great interest. Internally, it dates from at least the 17th century, for in a room upstairs there is a Jacobean ceiling, and its later history is detailed on a sign on the outside. In the early 18th century it was refronted, and although Wood professed to despise these early, highly ornamented buildings, he must have been influenced by them, for here again, climbing centrally, are the three orders of architecture, just as we find on Wood's later Circus. In fact, they are more correctly executed here. The whole lot is topped by a broken pediment – which does not mean it should be repaired, simply that the triangle above the window has a piece missing in the middle. Further along from the pub is a first-floor window with an attractive design in coloured glass. Take the next lane on the left, Parsonage Lane, and notice immediately on your left a pair of little cherubs over a blocked window, and a blocked archway further along. Wood says there were houses in Westgate Street "more like Mansions for Persons of Rank and Fortune, than for common Town Dwellings" and it is likely that this is a relic of one of them. Continue to the top of Parsonage Lane, cross the street, stand by the piece of city wall, and look back at the building to the right of the lane. This is the Victorian extension to the *Mineral Water Hospital*, and it is here, rather than in Wood's own building on the other side of the lane, that part of his design was finally fulfilled. He had always wanted to have a carving representing the Good Samaritan in the pediment, but the Royal Coat of Arms was substituted, not only politically tactful but cheaper (Ralph Allen was a Trustee). In the Victorian period, the age of grand philanthropic gestures, the Good Samaritan finally found his way into the pediment of the extension, where he can be seen, complete with donkey, sculpted by Henry Ezard and influenced by the original designs. Beyond the hospital can be seen the Jacobethan chimneys and French chateau spirelet of the Bluecoat School, rebuilt in 1859. Much derided by purists, it is a wonderful collection of all the various styles influencing architects at that period. It is, in fact, a bit of fun.

Turn and go down the slope behind you into Trim Street. You are forced to turn left, and on your right you will see what is known as *Wolfe's House*, since he stayed here with his parents in 1757. Locals surely will not need to be reminded of the carving in the pediment of the door, a memorial to the famous General. However, not many people notice the house to its right, where the owner has had some philosophical thoughts about doorbells. Go right under the archway, sometimes known, incorrectly, as Trim Bridge, and continue up Queen Street. You will, of course, notice that you are leaving St. Michael's Parish and entering Walcot! You didn't? You missed the parish boundary marks. On reaching Quiet Street at the end, cross, and if you were unaware that Bath has an extract from the Magna Carta, walk up John Street where you will find it, painted on the wall of the modern building to your left. See if you can find the good news it contained for widows. Returning to Quiet Street, look eastwards and you will see on the right-hand side a large building with three statues, one on each side of the central window and one on top. This is the Bazaar built in 1824 and attributed to Goodridge. It is said to be influenced by the Choragic Monument of Thrasyllus at Athens, which was frequently used as a model by the Greek Revival architects. The original, however, does not have Commerce and Genius, for that is what the two on the wall represent. The sculptor, Lucius Gahagan, seems to have given Genius an itchy stomach. What the third one at the top is, no-one seems to know, but the seagulls find him a convenient perch.

At the far end of Quiet Street is Milsom Street, with the entrance to Green Street almost opposite. Before crossing over to it, look to your right. The 'island' block has a marble cherub in a niche, which you may recognise, for it was rescued from the Melfort Cross, whose picture you saw at the *Cross Bath*. There is also a Royal Coat of Arms. Now cross into Green Street, an early 18th-century street built over an old bowling green. Like Broad Street, it has a fine mixture of transitional styles, as Palladio's designs found their way into local builders' pattern books. To the left is a gabled house with a fine shell doorway, and further down on the right, No.14 is an amateurish attempt to impose classically-inspired detail on a narrow gabled house. It has been an art shop and framers since the last century, and one owner proved his wood-carving skills by decorating the shop window with flowers and foliage. On reaching Broad Street, turn left, pass the old King Edward's School building before taking the little alleyway two shops above it. This was once one of the narrow entries into a court, like those described in 'Street of Strangers', but now takes you into a car park (where you should turn right). Once it was a stable yard, used by the Post Office at No.8 and the York House, whose stables can still be seen beneath the old hotel, complete with the rings between the doors where the horses would be tied up. It later became a livery stables and on the eastern side there were offices, living accommodation, and a drying room where the coachmen could hang their greatcoats. As you leave, using the archway at the top on the right, you will see the word 'Office' on your right, all that is left of the thriving business that once filled this yard. At the street end of the arch, notice the 'touchstones' on each side, to bounce carriages away from the wall.

Cross the road and take Broad Street Place, slightly down to the right. You have already visited this, so you might think there is nothing to detain us as we walk straight through to the steps on the far side, but ahead of you are traces of the old buildings in Walcot Street. There is a fine assortment of old chimney pots to right and left, and although the steps need to be descended with care, do not miss the little Cotswold-style window in the wall to your right. Turn right at the bottom, cross Saracen Street and walk past *The Saracen's Head* to *St. Michael's Church.* If you look across to *The Podium*, you will see above the supermarket window a piece of modern carving. This seems a very odd place to put an interesting piece of work, for few can ever notice it. The sculptor, Barry Baldwin, has included figures representing many aspects of Bath's history. Cross to *The Podium* and walk towards the *Abbey*, but turn left down Bridge Street. If you look across at the *Victoria Art Gallery* on the other side, you will see a statue of the queen herself, although Her Imperial Majesty seems to have had a sex change! She stands over a doorway in the keystone of which is a Valkyrie looking rather troubled, and well she might in view of her headwear.

Walk down to *Pulteney Bridge* to cross the road. Then take Grand Parade which takes you back towards Orange Grove. When the road swings round to the right you are in a good position to turn round and look at the *Empire Hotel*. When Bathonians have nothing else to argue about, this will always get them going. Should it stay or should it go? The main talking point is the unusual roof-line, which represents a castle, a manor house, and a cottage, but few seem to remember that at sometime in the last fifty years it has been toned down. The castle battlements had spiky decorations, the manor house had a shell carving at the top, with vases balanced on that: even the cottage was more fanciful. Despite the pleas of architects to be allowed to replace it with something less overwhelming, many local people seem to be saying "Better the devil we know". It is sometimes called Major Davis's Revenge. There is no doubt that he was treated abominably by the Council. One episode was described by the local paper as "a black page in the annals of the city; the interests of the citizens ... have been sacrificed to gratify personal pique." It was therefore understandable of Davis to build this mammoth enterprise right on the Guildhall's doorstep, and on which he was careful to sign his name. His initials, CD, can be seen in the canopy at the door.

It is perhaps appropriate to end this book with the *Empire Hotel*. First of all it is not Georgian, and although Bath looks back to that era with nostalgia, it was merely a century in 2,000 years of the city's history. Secondly, it is no bad thing to end on a note of controversy. Local history is never static: as more lost documents surface, so cherished theories have to be abandoned or fought for. If you are a Bath resident, I hope this book will sharpen your interest in this fascinating city, and if you are a visitor, perhaps it will inspire you to find out more about *your* home. Qualified historians do not have a monopoly on new discoveries. Who knows: it could be you who uncovers some facts which cause books to be rewritten!